TAP DANCING
in **Z***en*

TAP DANCING
in Zen

GERI LARKIN

CELESTIALARTS
Berkeley, California

Celestial Arts
P.O. Box 7123
Berkeley, California 94707

Distributed in Canada by Ten Speed Canada, in the United
Kingdom and Europe by Airlift Books, in New Zealand by
Southern Publishers Group, in Australia by Simon & Schuster
Australia, in South Africa by Real Books, and in Singapore,
Malaysia, Hong Kong, and Thailand by Berkeley Books.

Cover and interior design by Greene Design
Cover photograph by Chantra Pramkaew

Library of Congress Catalog Card Number: 99-75905

First printing, 2000
Printed in the United States

1 2 3 4 5 6 7 8 — 03 02 01 00 99

Dedication

꙳

This book is dedicated to Sarth Robert Larkin, a bodhisattva for the millennium.

I also bow in gratitude to my teachers, Venerable Samu Sunim and Kaju Linda Murray, and to the sangha that nourishes me every day. May all beings find peace.

Deep bows of gratitude I also make to the following people:

David Hinds for believing in me without compromise right up to his death; his spunky and compassionate colleagues Veronica Randall and Heather Garnos; Andrea Pedolsky for her constant graceful support; my family, all of them; my friends without number, especially Joy, Shala, Alice, Mak, all the Debras, Cheryl, David, and the most amazing crop of dharma students ever.

Contents

ﷻ

Preface

꽃

You know how you hear a song and for some inexplicable reason one of its lines is lodged permanently in your brain? For me, it was a line from an old Beach Boys song, "Rhonda," that would pop up whenever my brain was on hold. Like Dave Barry, I was sure the line was "Since you let me down there've been owls puking in my bed." So you can imagine my relief when someone recently told me those weren't the real words. And yes, I'm afraid I'm one of those people who thought the words to another great oldie were "'Scuse me while I kiss this guy."

Spiritual practice has helped me hear words more clearly, luckily for me and everyone around me who has to put up with my constant singing to myself. But lines still stick. For several years now there is a line from a song my friend Nat Needle wrote that seems to be with me day and night. It is this: "Seated in the cave of the heart find freedom." It comes from a passage in *The Dhammapada*, a collection of teachings of the Buddha. The full text is breathtaking:

As the master whittles,
And makes straight his arrows,
So the master directs his straying thoughts.

Like a fish out of water, stranded on the shore,
Thoughts thrash and quiver.
For how can they shake off desire?

They tremble, they are unsteady, they wander at their will.
It is good to control them,
And to master them brings happiness.
With single mindedness
The master quells his thoughts.
He ends their wandering.
Seated in the cave of the heart,
He finds freedom.

(*The Dhammapada: The Sayings of the Buddha,* translated
by Thomas Byrom, New York: Vintage Books, 1976)

For a long time I thought of the line as simply a lovely statement. Today I know it to be truth. Seated in the cave of our hearts is freedom. And the knowing makes me laugh out loud. All those years I spent getting overeducated, overmanicured, overhoused, overautomated, overeverythinged in an effort to find personal peace. While all the time I've been carrying freedom—in the form of pure happiness—in the cave of my heart. This must be one of the great cosmic jokes of our time.

We all have this freedom. The question is, how can we find the key, or keys, that will open our internal doors so we can all share in this knowing? My bet is that the sutras are those keys. *Sutras* are spiritual teachings in the form of strings of words that ancient seekers memorized and recited over and over as they sought enlightenment. They offered protection and guidance. Primal light sabers. And they worked. A person could pick one and concentrate on its offerings for a lifetime, grateful for its gifts.

In a world crammed with infobits, spiritual gurus, cable channels, email, and talk shows, there is, I think, a genuine thirst for simplicity, for finding a few simple tools for living fulfilled lives. One mate. One path. One teacher. One teaching. One sutra.

In the Buddhist tradition, practitioners are constantly advised—nagged is more like it—to spend our lives in four "sublime abodes." One is compassion, or *karuna*. Another is *mudita,* or sympathetic joy. A third is equanimity, or *upekka*. The fourth is love, *metta*. Without love, compassion

erodes into contempt and sympathetic joy morphs into self-satisfaction.
Equanimity becomes heartless indifference. We deserve better.

So a primary task of serious spiritual seekers is to cultivate love—
spiritual love: friendliness, benevolence, care, and concern. One sutra
that shows you and me how to get there from wherever we are is the
Metta Sutra, or the sutra of loving-kindness. Here is a version of it:

This is what should be done
By one who is skilled in goodness,
And who knows the path of peace:
Let them be able and upright,
Straightforward and gentle in speech.
Humble and not conceited,
Contented and easily satisfied.
Unburdened with duties and frugal in their ways.
Peaceful and calm, and wise and skillful,
Not proud and demanding in nature.
Let them not do the slightest thing
That the wise would later reprove.
Wishing: in gladness and in safety,
May all beings be at ease.
Whatever living beings there may be;
Whether they are weak or strong, omitting none,
The great or the mighty, medium, short, or small,
The seen and the unseen,
Those living near and far away,
Those born and to-be-born—
May all beings be at ease!
Let none deceive another,
Or despise any being in any state,
Let none through anger or ill will
Wish harm upon another.
Even as a mother protects with her life
Her child, her only child,

So with a boundless heart
Should one cherish all living beings;
Radiating kindness over the entire world:
Spreading upwards to the skies,
And downwards to the depths;
Outward and unbounded,
Freed from hatred and ill will.
Whether standing or walking, seated or lying down
Free from drowsiness,
One should sustain this recollection.

Some people believe, and I am one of them, that this sutra is, in its own perfect way, a pure rendition of not just the Buddha's teachings on love, but also of the guidelines that lead us directly into the cave of our hearts—into the peace and joy that is our natural birthright. It is the Zen light that shows us the path we are trying to find.

Throughout the past year this sutra has been the mother lode that I have mined for dharma talks at the Ann Arbor, Chicago, and Toronto Zen Buddhist temples. Now chapters of this book, the talks represent one woman's effort to bring this sutra of boundless love alive in our time, so we can mine it together. On our neurotic days we can mine it neurotically. On our compassionate days we can mine it compassionately. On our angry days we can be dragons ripping it to shreds in our teeth. No matter what our state of mind, it will work.

While I studied this and other sutras almost daily over the past year, I realized that they offer us the universe on a plate. It comes in the form of freedom from all the fears that haunt us. This, in turn, allows us to open to a deeper understanding of the sheer brilliance of the universe you and I happen to be inhabiting these days. Since I can't jump out of the page in joy (yet) and beg you to strive harder, concentrate more, and pay deeper attention, *Tap Dancing in Zen* is my offering. Its stories and insights have been rendered from the parts of me that are wiser, though still somewhat ego-encrusted. You've been stumbling long enough, dear reader and fellow seeker, it's time to start walking.

※

On Finding the Path of Peace

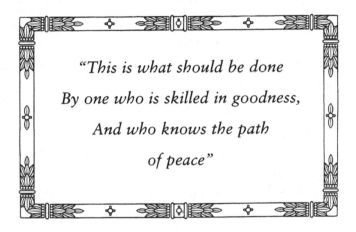

> *"This is what should be done*
> *By one who is skilled in goodness,*
> *And who knows the path*
> *of peace"*

Trail markers definitely help. Without them I know I would have been lost on every trail I've ever hiked—even the ones where I could see my car in the distance. There is just something utterly confusing about the woods to this city dweller. I have always been grateful for these little signs that I was on the right path. They gave me the energy to keep going and erased the fear that I would be spending an unplanned night in the woods.

We all need such trail markers. In this modern life of sleep deprivation, caffeine overload, and chronic anxiety we need to know that we're still on the path to peace—and that we'll make it eventually. In Buddhism, sutras are the markers. As the tradition moved from its homebase in northern India to other countries, the teachings were passed from person to person in the form of prose poems. Usually quite long, they are believed to have been delivered originally either by Buddha himself or by a great teacher speaking under Buddha's inspiration. Think of them as Buddhist gospels.

Their sole purpose was to awaken in the person hearing them their Buddha nature, or what the teacher Sangharakshita calls our transcendental intuition. The sutras make the Buddha's teachings clear enough for listeners to both understand and act on them: "In seeing the peach blossoms, there is enlightenment to the way; in hearing the echo of bamboo there is enlightenment to the way; in seeing the morning star, there is enlightenment to the way. Sutras help people of wisdom to grow... such sutras are the whole world in ten directions, which is nothing but sutras." (Kogen Mizuno, *Buddhist Sutras: Origin, Development, and Transmission*, Tokyo, Japan: Kosei Publishing Co., 1982)

The sutras are weavings of important sayings that were originally carried in the minds and hearts of elder monks who had unlocked their hearts through their spiritual practice. There may be as many as 84,000, some written down, but mostly passed along from memory. Because the sutras represent the core teachings of Buddha, many Buddhists believe that simply reciting them brings merit to the reciter and bestows grace on those who hear the words—something to remember if you ever feel the need to bring some grace into a business meeting or tough situation. Just thinking the words of the sutra may help.

The first person to recite sutras after Buddha's death some 2,500 years ago was Ananda, his cousin and attendant. When Buddha's followers convened to discuss what they should do next, Ananda, renowned for his extraordinary memory, proceeded to recite everything he had ever heard the Buddha teach. The monks, sorting through Ananda's monologue, decided that the best way to hold on to Buddha's compassionate wisdom was to frame his teachings into the form of long poems they could remember and thus carry with them throughout India and later on to China, Japan, other parts of Asia, and eventually into the

Western world. Over time other sutras were added to the collection by a wide range of great masters, from Huineng to Dogen.

The Metta Sutra, which has been attributed to the Buddha himself, shines in its simplicity and dignity. Its core lessons? Simple—if we hold onto our humility, if we let go of our egos and stop clinging to whatever it is we're clinging to, we'll find the wonderful surprise that behind all that gunk is a natural kindness, a love for everyone and everything that we never thought we had. And if we let ourselves act from that place, we'll discover a kindness without limits and an unutterable peace.

The practice of loving-kindness has a way of morphing into a sort of spontaneous compassion, into generosity and a willingness to be open to everything and to do whatever is called for in the moment, in any situation. It inspires in me a sort of fearlessness. Opened wide by loving-kindness, I am not afraid to trust my own heart, even if what I do results in someone else's disregard. On my best days, a generosity of spirit bubbles up and with it a deep willingness to just be in a given situation. Life becomes more improvisational, less planned. The need for rules disappears because every situation calls for a different response. I have learned to lean harder on principles and values. When I act from compassion, things tend to work out. This is part of the reason why spiritual teachers in the Zen tradition hesitate to speak in truisms, knowing that each moment has its own truth. This explains why a Zen teacher can tell one student that she is right about a particular teaching and turn right around and tell a different student that he is also right, even though he may have a completely different interpretation. Our worlds are different. The world changes in an instant. None of us is safe.

My teacher Samu Sunim teaches that we will be okay in any situation if we just do three things: 1. Don't panic. 2. Assess the situation. 3. Do the obvious. There are no rules to follow. If I manifest the loving-kindness in my heart, I will know what needs to be done. So will you.

A while ago, I had a pretty tough year. It was a lousy, gritty, I-feel-sorry-for-myself, the-world-is-going-to-hell-in-a-handbasket, and where-did-this-extra-twenty-pounds-come-from-anyway kind of year. It was a year without television and a year I lived with a teenager who had decided that swimming was her life, which necessitated getting up at 5 A.M. and spending weekends at various pools around the state of Michigan. It was a year with a car that would randomly stop of its own accord. It was the year I drove over an animal and killed it, and for one teensy moment wished it was my ex-husband—the mean one. It was the year I discovered that I had somehow grown a mustache. It was a sucky, head-under-the-pillow, get-me-some-chocolate, stop-calling-me-after-8:30-P.M.-because-I'm-in-bed-and-have-no-life year.

I recited the Metta Sutra every morning when my eyes first opened, before going to the bathroom and doing prostrations and meditating. "This is what should be done by one who is skilled in goodness and who knows the path of peace...." And learned some of the deepest lessons of my life: that loving-kindness is a cosmic bottom line, and that life isn't about pushing anything away. It's about embracing the whole damn mess.

I realized that I could make peace with my parents—whoever they are, whatever they did. I just had to let go of my resentments, my anger, my annoyance, my desire to punish them, my need to blame. It's so simple: Just stop. Let go. If I'm filled with only one thing at a time, and if that thing is loving-kindness, then there is no room for resistance or anger or the rest of those snotty-nosed kid emotions we all thrive on. No room for those emotions that suck enormous quantities of energy right out of us, the ones that make us sick and crabby and needy.

I realized that wanting to live a life filled with loving-kindness meant **being** loving-kindness. When I'm miserable it's because I make myself miserable. Suffering really is a choice. And even if I'm still crazy after all these years—or angry, or timid, or jealous—at the bottom of that anger and fear and jealousy everything is really okay. I just need to remember so I can let go of the craziness.

The Metta Sutra taught me that spiritual practice isn't about getting better at anything. Rather it's about appreciating everything and being my own best friend.

In reciting or chanting the Metta Sutra or even simply thinking it through, and then sitting quietly, all sorts of insights about ourselves are revealed. It's as though we're looking in some sort of cosmic mirror. Metta is about learning how we tick, why we do the silly things we do as well as the wonderful things we do. As understanding grows our addiction to our ego-self falls away. We stop obsessing about why this happened or why that didn't happen, and clinging to our emotional wounds—at least I did.

Expectations also fall away. Only openness remains. And you know what? If we don't expect anything we don't get impatient or disappointed. Instead we experience real pleasure in the simple, everyday situations. Joy starts to trickle up through our hardened arteries—because it finally can. Every day begins to feel like a day at Disney World.

The power of this sutra leaves me breathless.

Heidi Singh is a woman who has been practicing meditation for over twenty-five years. When her father, an alcoholic, was dying of lung cancer that had spread to his bones, he basically shifted between two emotions, anger and bitterness.

Heidi felt hopeless to help this difficult man who had abandoned her family years before. But her teacher assured her that if she practiced loving-kindness toward her father each day as he was dying, things would improve.

So she did. She stuck with her practice and stuck with her father. And it moved emotional mountains. First it gave her patience and understanding. Then it opened her heart wide open. She was able to see her father as a tragic person whose life had been consumed by a suffering so great that he had lost his ability to love. Eventually a deep love that had been hidden in her heart for years began to surface.

Here's the best part: On the day her father died, Heidi spontaneously asked him if she could recite a Buddhist prayer for him. He agreed. She recited the Heart Sutra, which has at its core a teaching that all phenomenal forms—chairs, rugs, woods, tears—are really empty of anything except our own projections of meaning. When we let go of these meanings what we find is the awakened heart. As Heidi whispered the sutra into her father's ear, tears streamed down his face and she was able, finally, to tell him how much she loved him and how grateful she was for all the good things he had done for her. She promised to pray for him always. Then, in the moment before he died, though he could not speak, he mouthed the words "I love you." This is the power of Metta Sutra. It is the path of peace that lets us live our lives in neutral, protected by a deep trust in ourselves.

When I was in my early thirties, I worked for a brilliant man who threw the most spectacular tantrums of anyone I've known before or since. Which is saying a lot, since I was married to a champion tantrum-thrower for years. There's just something about seeing a grown man fling himself to the ground and pound it with his fist because he isn't getting what he wants that just blows my mind. Anyway, this former boss used to throw things too. Reports. Books. One day he threw some at me. Stunned and in tears, I left the office and went home to decide what to do. I loved the work I was doing. I felt it was my calling. And I adored my colleagues. They were smart and compassionate; they were like family. I even adored my boss, except for the tantrum part. I paced into the night that night. One moment I was determined never to go back, and the next I was on the verge of forgiving him. Then it would go back to "What a jerk!" and then tears at the thought of having to quit. I'm sure you've been there.

Finally I called Katie, a colleague with whom he had never been angry. She was a quiet, kind woman, not one of the firm's obvious leaders. Always unruffled. Always smiling. I told her what had happened and asked her what she would do. Silence. Finally, "When there is nothing to shoot at, how can he aim?" Okay, at the time I had no idea what she meant, but her voice was comforting enough for me to go back to work for another year. It took me years, in fact, to understand what she meant. It took the loving-kindness and the emptiness the Metta Sutra offers. In *Buddhism Through American Women's Eyes*, Tsering Everest explains Katie's message more skillfully than I ever could: "When someone makes you angry, it is as if they shot an arrow at your heart. It doesn't hit you but lands right at your foot. Then you pick up the arrow and stab yourself with it over and over again. That's what happens. Anything in life can be the cause of getting upset, but the choice to be upset or not is our own." (*Buddhism Through American Women's Eyes*, edited by Karma Lekshe Tsomo, Ithaca, N.Y.: Snow Lion Publications, 1995)

Thinking back, I probably drove the guy nuts, not that his tantrums were ever okay. I remembered that I argued all the time, rarely listened, and always tried to position myself as having the only moral solution to any problem that surfaced, which made him the bad guy no matter what. I needed to be right and I needed to be right in the most arrogant way possible. And while throwing things at someone else would not be a personal choice for demonstrating frustration, I now understand the motivation a little better.

Metta helps us spot the muck in our lives before it hardens into concrete. In the spaciousness it offers, life can truly be lived moment by moment. Life just doesn't get any better. In this mindful mode we can, finally, keep an eagle eye on our minds so we don't end up wasting precious time with toxic thoughts. After all, if we won't eat rotten food, why should we think rotten thoughts? Of course, stress will always be around. But we don't have to react to every stressful event that comes our way. We can shrug things off, let them go, deal with what needs dealing with and move on.

At a snail's pace and with a thousand miles of backsliding along the way, I have learned this: Without loving-kindness in our hearts, peace is impossible. Any peace. When there is no metta we are wasting our lives. Drowning in *samsara* (the indefinitely repeated cycles of birth, life, and death caused by karma). Don't let it happen. Remember that we all want peace really. We don't want pain.

Where to start with metta? Try just being curious. Be curious about your own life. Be wildly watchful the way a two-year-old is. Investigate these teachings of the Buddha, of other saints, of Jesus and Muhammad. Be curious about sutras. Be curious about how reciting a sutra over and over again can have a profound impact on your life. Read the sutras to find the one that reaches the most deeply into your heart. Not your mind, your heart. Then read it with your heart. And remember to watch for markers on your spiritual path. They'll be there. I know because your guardian angel told me.

Chapter One

It's About the Words That Come Out of Our Mouths

> "*Let them be able and upright,*
>
> *Straightforward*
>
> *and gentle in speech*"

In Buddha's eightfold path out of suffering, right speech is smack in the middle. It is one of three cornerstones of moral practice. The other two are right action and right livelihood, or how we make our livings. Moral practice, *shila*, is about backing away not just from actions but also words that harm others. This matters not only because of their impact on other people, but also because of their impact on us. When we insult someone or yell at them, our own minds are deeply agitated, and inside that agitation is either craving or aversion. Craving to be right, to be stronger, to get even. Aversion in the form of dislike, hate, disgust, anger. In this mind state it is impossible, literally *impossible*, to be happy. Instead, not only are we causing suffering, we are reinforcing the very mental habits we've been trying to get rid of. It's a hell realm and we've landed smack in the middle of it, and our words got us there.

I sometimes work at a shelter for victims of domestic violence called HAVEN, which is located in Pontiac, Michigan. While Pontiac may not be the epicenter of domestic violence in this country, it would probably make the short list. The stories the staff tell about the women who stay there leave me numb.

I believe that these stories can stop, that the vision of a world without domestic violence is possible. HAVEN's long-term goal is to put itself out of business by ending domestic violence. Its strategic starting point? Taking on abusive speech.

Because it is such a powerful trigger for violence, the end of harmful speech can have an extraordinary impact. Professionals in the field of domestic violence regularly focus on the harm done by speech—on put-downs and angry words, and the terror that comes from being shouted at. When you walk into HAVEN's office the first thing you see is a large black and white poster on the wall. A little girl's face looks back at you. You can only see half of it because half is in shadows. She is beautiful. Huge black eyes with curly tendrils of hair around her cheeks. Maybe she is four years old. Maybe she is your daughter. Or you. Above her face, in her own handwriting, the poster pleads with us to "stop words that hurt." Here are the words on the bottom of the poster: "Start using words that help. Words can hit a child as hard as a fist. And leave scars that last a lifetime. Even when you're upset...stop! Think about what you're saying." (National Committee to Prevent Child Abuse, Box 2866P, Chicago, IL 60690)

Words matter. They need to be kind and clear, straightforward and gentle. The Metta Sutra reminds us of this. Gentle speech is more than just the absence of anger. It is also about telling the truth, and refraining from spreading rumors, or making fun of someone else, or even meaningless chatter, one of my all-time favorite pastimes! These are all forms of speech that can harm us, that can knock us off our spiritual path.

Right speech. The Buddha explained it this way: One who practices right speech "speaks the truth and is steadfast in truthfulness, trustworthy, dependable, straightforward with others. He reconciles the quarreling and encourages the united. He delights in harmony, seeks after harmony, rejoices in harmony, and creates harmony by his words. His speech is gentle, pleasing to the ear, kindly, heartwarming, courteous, agreeable, and enjoyable to many. He speaks at the proper time, according to the facts, according to what is helpful, according to the Dharma and the Code of Conduct. His words are worth remembering, timely, well-reasoned, well-chosen, and constructive." (S. N. Goenka, "Moral Conduct, Concentration, and Wisdom," in *Entering the Stream: An Introduction to the Buddha and His Teachings,* edited by Samuel Bercholz and Sherab Chodzin Kohn, Boston: Shambhala Publications, 1993, pp. 98–99)

So how do we practice right speech? Well, we can be more straightforward so people don't have to guess what we really mean. And we can take the time to be clear. I have learned, over time, that fewer words are almost always better. When I think of straightforward speech I think of my friend Alice. She is one of my very best friends for a lot of reasons. Mostly because she says things to me that nobody else will. When I called her to tell her after years of determined celibacy that I had fallen in love with a young hunk, she just sighed and said in her best-friend voice, "Sooner or later one of you will walk away and it will really hurt." In a single sentence she forced me to take a radically honest look at where I was headed. Was this something that could deepen my practice or did I want to be just like Stella getting my groove back? I thanked Alice, even though I hated hearing what she was saying, and felt a surge of gratefulness for a friend who could make her points and ask her questions without feeling the need to belittle me, or him.

Hanging up, I sat down to do some guided meditation. Thich Nhat Hanh's "Looking Deeply, Letting Go" came to mind because it has a capacity for piercing all my protective shells when I don't want to look at something in my life directly. Here is a version:

Contemplating the attractive body of a man,
I breathe in.
Seeing the impermanent nature of that body, I breathe out.

Contemplating the danger that my craving for sex can bring about,
I breathe in.
Letting go of the craving,
I breathe out.

Contemplating the suffering that my craving for sex can bring about,
I breathe in.
Letting go of the craving,
I breathe out.

Contemplating the hardship that my craving for sex can bring about,
I breathe in.
Letting go of the craving,
I breathe out.

(Thich Nhat Hanh, *The Blooming of a Lotus: Guided Meditation Exercises for Healing and Transformation*, Boston: Beacon Press, 1993)

Sitting, I could feel a real happiness sweep through my body as I realized that, aside from the sex part, I really, really cared about this person, and was thrilled that we had tripped over each other in this lifetime. I vowed to be careful. And gentle. I vowed to offer up the best part of me to the relationship, to thank the skies for a friend like Alice who uses words with such skill and compassion, and to stick with my practice if things got tough.

The impact of words. My daughter now plays water polo. She seems to like it because she keeps going to practice. Her coach says she has improved dramatically since she started. All I know is that every time I go to a game and she comes out of the pool without exploded eardrums or broken limbs, I'm happy.

This year the team had a new coach, only slightly older than the players. Although she was more of a sister to them, still, she rode the

players hard for the whole season. But just before the state champi-
onships, she told the team's parents she wasn't sure if the team could
make seventh place—out of seven teams. Despite all the months of hard
work, the team just hadn't pulled together.

Then, through a series of surprising upsets, the young women managed to literally scratch their way up to second place. Suddenly they
were face to face with a monster team that tends to win water polo
matches by huge margins, typically 14 to 3.

At the start of the play-off game the coach was standing with the
team, all of them discouraged. They had barely made it through the first
quarter. There had been too many mistakes: overshooting, undershoot-
ing, being at the wrong place at the right time—you name it. As they
stood there not knowing how to react to the situation, a group of friends
and parents lifted a huge banner in the stands. On it was one word:
"Believe."

And I'll be damned if they didn't kick butt after that. Because they
dared to believe that they could actually win the championship. And
they almost did, with everyone in the stands—even all the other
teams—screaming for them at the top of their lungs. Those young
women came out of that game as one great storybook team. All on the
strength of a word.

Simple words melt hearts. Think of when someone has said, "I love
you." These three words can break us wide open. I can't hear them without tearing up, including when they are directed at someone else.

And yet, we're afraid of fewer, simpler words. I'm not sure why.
Maybe we feel too naked, too exposed. But we need to practice, because
fewer words offer listeners space where they can settle in to what is being
said. Buddha was a master of this form of communication. Instead of lec-
turing on and on about how we need to be responsible for ourselves and
giving us all the reasons why, he said, "Be a lamp unto yourself." Boom.
That's it. When there are fewer words it is hard to run away from whatever is being said. Instead of endless instructions about how we should
live our lives, he says, "Live in joy. In peace." Crisp and clear.

If we aren't, we know it is time to uncover all those neuroses and obsessions to see where we need to do some mental vacuum cleaning. Occasionally, usually during a walking meditation, I'll ask myself, "So, woman, are you living in joy?" Happily the answer is usually affirmative. But when it isn't, I'll take some time to do a form of Vipassana meditation practice, where I ask myself, "What is getting in the way?" and just sit there watching what surfaces. The list of reasons is usually pretty silly. Sometimes my old Honda needs a ton of work and I don't have ready cash. Or I'll be half in love with someone and can't quite decide whether to do anything about it.

Straightforward and gentle speech. I love that about this spiritual path. We don't have to guess at things. Using simple, gentle words as a springboard, we can dive right into our own muck to see what keeps dragging us under. In gentleness we can do the work that needs doing, rediscovering the joy that is ours.

For backup, role models exist all around us. An Indian woman currently living in Thalheim, Germany, Mother Meera is experienced by many spiritual seekers as an avatar, a living embodiment of the Divine Mother. What always strikes me as I think about her is how fully she embodies "straightforward and gentle in speech." In a beautiful story describing his relationship with Mother Meera, her student Andrew Harvey tells of how he kept running away from Mother, only to come back, only to run away again and come back again. I remember occasionally being consumed with the same urges during my seminary years, which is why his relationship to Mother is so moving to me. Once after running away for eight years, Andrew telephoned Mother out of the blue:

> "Can I come and stay in your house?"
> "You can stay as long as you like," she said.
> After the bitterness and horror of the previous years the warmth of her low voice brought tears to my eyes, and for a brief while I could not speak....
> "I have been away from you for a long time."

"You have always been with me."

A long pause, then her voice came, very young and gentle.

"Are you coming this Friday?"

(Andrew Harvey, *Hidden Journey: A Spiritual Awakening,* New York: Viking Penguin, 1992)

It is her words, her simple, love-filled words that heal him. She tells Andrew, "As you awaken, all those you love awaken a little with you. All those you love are linked by that love, are on the same spiral, rising... the Divine never forces. The ego forces. The Divine is patient." (*Hidden Journey,* p. 196)

Straightforward and gentle in speech. A few months ago I was in Toronto for a weekend at the Zen Buddhist temple. My teacher, Venerable Samu Sunim, wasn't there but called me from the road to ask me to write down my measurements for some new fancy robes he was ordering. In a rush to get home before midnight, I grabbed a woman as I ran out the door and literally stood in the middle of the hall while she quickly took my measurements, and I hurriedly wrote them down on a scrap of paper. I left the paper in the office and tore back to Ann Arbor. About halfway home I realized that I had been deeply disrespectful to Sunim in my rushing. I wasn't even sure the measurements were correct since we hadn't double-checked ourselves. I had written them in such sloppy handwriting, there was a good chance he wouldn't even be able to read what I had written. I thought about turning around and decided not to, justifying my decision by saying to myself that turning around would waste precious resources—namely gas.

The next day Sunim called and said only two sentences: "I have your measurements. They are insincere." It was a whack across my head. He was right! I had been insincere. I had resisted and wanted to do what I wanted to do, instead of paying attention to the situation and giving it everything I had. He had lots of reasons to yell, to lecture, but instead Sunim only said those two things and hung up. And I vowed never again to be so casual.

Straightforward and gentle in speech. If Mother Meera can, we can. And if Sunim does, I'd better.

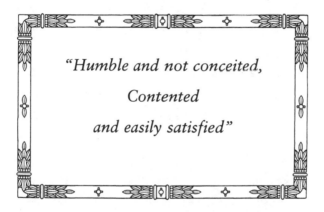

Humility
as Joy

"Humble and not conceited,

Contented

and easily satisfied"

We all long for joy. Some of us strive for what we think will bring us joy so intensely that we will sacrifice anything and everything to get to it. Take the workaholics in my life: if we just *have* a little more, *do* a little more. There is one more deal to be made, one more room to build, an extra report that I could finish before tomorrow, a speech that will make me better known and richer.

If we're lucky (yes—lucky), some catastrophe will knock us right off this tail-chasing track. Maybe we'll be lucky enough to lose our job, or a race, or our house, or our money. And at the very moment that we feel like a failure, we are given an extraordinary opportunity to learn the truth about joy: Joy is never in the stuff of our lives, nor is it in the opinions of others or wanting to think we're special. Humility is what allows us to live our lives fully, giving each moment the attention it deserves. Humility is the absence of greed or desire, of wanting things we don't have and probably don't need.

People often look surprised whenever I mention that *Fortune* is one of my favorite magazines. It is right up there with *People, The Utne Reader,* and *Fast Company* for its readability and world view. Having said this, I don't know if I would keep subscribing if Stanley Bing ever stopped writing for the magazine. A corporate executive at an unnamed Fortune 500 company, Bing openly struggles with the perils that come with worldly success in a way that is both moving and, at times, hysterically funny. In one of his recent essays, "The Spirit Is Willing," Bing eloquently spears egotism as he searches for a way to fill the aching spiritual void between "dinner and the end of the millennium."

One evening Bing is watching the news, since, as you know, nothing fills an aching void quite as well as the news. On his screen a picture appears of a large group of men who are hollering and hugging and crying. Bing is riveted, not because of their obvious emotion, but because they aren't football players. Instead, glued to the screen, he discovers that they are Promise Keepers giving each other support as they each pledge to be more responsible to the people in their lives and to Jesus.

Bing is stunned. In a rush of insight he decides that he needs to find more meaning in his life. First he turns to spirituality:

I started with Buddhism. I've noticed many influential people are gravitating to it these days. Steven Seagal, the bad actor, was recently named a holy man by the Dalai Lama's people in Los Angeles, enabling him to channel the spirits of the ancient departed masters and also raise money. Richard Gere, of course, was in on the whole thing way before anybody else, but now you rarely see an entertainer who isn't hugging some lama or other at a chic benefit for Tibet hosted by Brad Pitt and his agent. I'd like to be with those people. So I tried to catch the Buddhist wave for a couple of days. It didn't work. You have to sit for hours and hours and think about nothing. I normally get paid for that. And there are no guarantees such contemplation will pay off in anything more than a certain quiet satisfaction. Me, I'm looking for ecstasy. So I moved on.

(Stanley Bing, "The Spirit Is Willing," *Fortune Magazine*, November 10, 1997)

Bing tries science. Still empty. So he decides to simply worship himself and his material success and proceeds to immerse himself in his work, which, in the fall of 1997, means getting his company's management information systems to a point at which they will survive the turn of the next century. At the end of the essay, Bing is digging right in, his taped glasses perched on the end of his nose, surrounded by "a group of wizened gnomes huddled over a computer monitor." ("The Spirit Is Willing") Empty, funny, but empty. Joyless, mostly, and he knows it.

My guess is that humility is just around Bing's next corner, offering up a path to happiness and a way to fill his void.

I honestly used to think that joy was directly correlated to the strength of orgasms. Time spent with a really gorgeous lover in Bali. That would do it. That's what the media taught me, and all the magazines I read over and over as I clawed my way through adolescence into adulthood. It was everywhere, this message. It still is.

Then, as I made my way through my thirties, I embraced a more complicated perspective. Joy was any orgasm plus a house and car I could brag about, two exotic vacations a year, and the ability to make thousands of dollars worth of charitable donations annually without blinking. Finally, in my forties, I've learned better. When I feel joy fly right up my spine and hover like a glow around me, it isn't from anything material. And it isn't from sex, even great sex. And contrary to an increasingly popular opinion that joy happens when we are able to fully express our feelings, my experience is different. It pops up whenever there is an absence of "me" and instead, an appreciation of whatever situation I am in, **whatever it is.** Even tough situations. When my experience is humility, my feeling is joy.

Here are the reasons: In those moments my mind is not trying to be right, to make me best, to be rich, to be thin. Instead, I can float in the timeless moment of now. It is so cool. Humility takes me across the river of my own ego to the land of acceptance of all that is, where we are each no better or worse off than everything else we find ourselves surrounded by on this merry-go-round we've labeled life.

When I don't have to defend myself—clinging to my need to be whatever it is I think I should be—amazing things happen. The first one is all the mind time freed up for spiritual work, since I'm not obsessing about what I should have, could have, or should have had. I'm not obsessing about what I'll do next. Instead, I'm hunkered down, giving each moment the best me I can, trusting that things really do take care of themselves if I just pay attention. And they always do.

Humility opens us up. It's as though we are looking and seeing with new eyes, through different lenses. We discover that there are teachers everywhere, and many ways to learn.

A while back I facilitated a half-day workshop at a local university for its leadership institute. The topic was "Balancing Your Life." One of the exercises was to make a collage to show what a balanced life would look like to each of the participants. Predictably people pasted pictures of families and friends onto their poster boards. Water was a big theme— beaches, pools. Nice houses, mostly big ones. Sports. Pictures of pets showed up. Two people had hot air balloon rides. Cigars in bed after sex—for both partners. When they were finished, each person was asked to stand in front of the group, collage in hand, and talk about what would guarantee him or her a balanced life, a happy life. One young woman, new to the university, knocked us all off our feet with her poster. Unlike the other collages, hers had very few pictures and few words. Instead, in big block letters she had written across the board, "I want to be the person my dog thinks I am." She had figured out how to tap into joy by petting and hugging and paying attention; by being responsible and making sure the people and pets around us are fed; by picking up the dog excrement in the middle of the living room without getting angry because we know no harm was meant; by spontaneously playing around with whatever happens to be within reach; and by always coming back.

It's a little scary that we aren't better at this stuff. I would certainly be much farther along my spiritual path if I were. I still find myself whipping out my doctorate whenever I am trying to make a point and feel like someone isn't listening to me with enough respect. And I continue to harbor this secret wish that someone will donate one of those new BMW convertibles to the temple so we can drive it around on our alms rounds. There are so many books crowding my little apartment that it feels half its size. A bigger one would work better. I still think about a recent job offer that was attached to a $120,000 base salary, and I still find myself gravitating toward the international travel magazines whenever I'm at Borders bookstore.

That's why spiritual practice matters as much as it does. Ego is a slippery slope, greased by desire. Without the sitting and chanting and prostrations, all that "wishing for" could still win out, even when my own experience has been an utter lack of joy as I wallowed in material success. Okay, there were moments. But that was all, just moments. Not even close to what cloaks me on most of my days these days. In the peace and calm of prayer I remember the point—to live each moment fully. Sitting at a window watching young ducklings try to pick apart a crust of bread, I remember the sheer beauty of the natural world, something I forgot in my material-girl years.

There are other gifts inside this one. Inside humility is a friendliness, a generic universal friendliness that also nourishes and protects us. A notion that human beings are all fundamentally good. This friendliness is a powerful weapon against the diseases of this society—the racism, the hate, the excruciating need to win at all costs. It inspires miracles. Here is just one example. Stephan Schwartz, a writer for magazines such as *National Geographic,* tells of a period in the early 1960s when he moved to Washington, D.C., to work for a powerhouse law firm. A full member of the insider's insider power network, the firm's prestige showed up in all sorts of ways. One was that each of the four elevators in its building had a human operator. Rosa was Stephan's favorite. A Puerto Rican woman no more than five feet tall, Rosa spoke very little English. But her friendliness, which she shared with anyone who entered her car in the form of a huge smile, could light up a person's entire day. Stephan would actually hover around the elevators until Rosa's would open, so he could see himself in her smile.

One day he found himself standing next to a senator about to vote against a bill that offered coal miners increased benefits for black lung disease. The bill also favored stringent work rules to protect them from more extreme work conditions. The senator had stopped by the law firm on his way to vote against the bill because one of its partners—a college classmate—had asked him to check in to see if there was any way to change the senator's mind.

The partner and senator met to no avail. Leaving for the Hill, the senator got into Rosa's elevator and proceeded to drop his pen: "It rolled to Rosa's feet, and she reached down and handed it back with one of her radiant smiles. He thanked her. She gave him another smile." (Stephan Schwartz, "The Elevator Ride," *New Age Journal,* November 1997, p. 176) Later that day the senator **voted for the miners.** People were amazed at his change of heart. When Stephan later caught up with an aide to find out what had happened, the aide told him that the senator, on his way to the Hill, had sat quietly in his car and then said, "You know if I vote against this, a lot of women like the elevator operator won't be smiling. Wives. Daughters. Nieces. Aunts. Maybe we need to rethink this." The senator returned to his office and called other senators to join him in changing their votes.

When we are humble everyone is a potential best friend and our generosity naturally grows. We want to do things, to help out. A wonderful Zen tradition is called *inji-gyo,* or secret good deeds. The virtue gained through performing a secret good deed is believed to be immense. So, in a monastery, if one watched closely, you might see a monk secretly mending another's robes or taking down someone's laundry and folding it before the rain comes. In our temple I often find chocolate spontaneously appearing in my mailbox, or a beautiful poem, unsigned. This year the Easter Bunny visited our Sunday service, leaving chocolate eggs under everyone's cushions, even the one prepared for a visiting Zen master. Sometimes the bathrooms are miraculously cleaned overnight. And flowers spontaneously appear in a neighbor's yard, thanks to the children in the temple. Secret good deeds. They are so much fun. In their doing you can't help but smile.

Finally there is this. Immersed in a sea of humility we realize that everything that happens to us is a secret good deed. I love the story of the little boy who tried out for a school play, determined to get a part in it. When his mother picked him up from school on the day the parts were announced, he rushed up to her filled with joy: "Guess what, Mom! I've been chosen to clap and cheer!"

Let's be on his team. Let's clap and cheer, forgetting the stage, knowing at last that real happiness comes from sitting in our seats enthralled with the play.

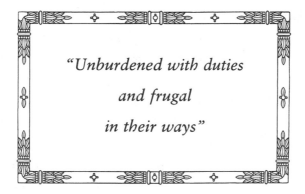

Chapter Three

Untangling Our Duties

> "Unburdened with duties
> and frugal
> in their ways"

July 22, 1998

Journal entry: "I am sitting at an old white metal desk in a cabin in the Catskills about four hours' drive northwest of New York City. Everywhere I look there is only nature. In front of me, mountains. Behind me, corn. On one side a field of wildflowers, and on the other, trees...big trees. The biggest trees I've ever seen outside of Northern California. I've rented the cabin for $9 a day and an hour of manual labor. Mostly that translates into stacking wood and cleaning up the various sheds on the property. Heat comes from a wood stove, an outhouse works for a toilet, and there is no hot water because I decided not to use the gas water heater.

"There is such peace in living this way. Two sets of clothing are enough, and I've discovered that living simply has meant I'm not hungry so much. Cereal and peanut butter toast, tofu, vegetables, and brown rice are plenty—and Starbucks Frappuccino because life without caffeine would just be too clean and I'm no saint. I wake up at 5 A.M. with the birds and go to sleep at night when they stop singing. Some days there is sun. Today, rain. Meditation practice makes up the bulk of each day—mostly sitting, sometimes walking. Occasionally it kicks itself in while I do manual work. I am my practice. After almost a week of this, it is hard to find 'me' in all of the spaciousness of a completely filled life. I've unburdened myself of my duties and, as the old song shouts, 'I feel good!'"

It was enough. A small cabin, about six different foods, two changes of clothes. No phone, no fax, no television. No computer, no email, no pager. No frantic phone calls, rescheduling of meetings, requests for speaking. Those weeks on the mountain taught me everything I needed to know about simplicity and living a full life. After a while I found myself scheming: How can I stay here forever? What do I need to do? And then I would spend hours thinking about how I would get rid of all the obligations in my life so I could be a permanent mountain ascetic.

What was this shift that was going on? Like most Americans, I was raised to take my place in this fast-paced, fast-talking, ever accomplishing, always moving world. Multiple obligations have become the adult merit badges of efficiency, and sometimes courage. "Ask a busy person if you want to get something done" is a national mantra. When someone asks us what we do, we don't say, "I do accounting," we say, "I am an accountant." Or "I am an architect" or "I am a plumber."

For those of us who try to have more than just a work identity, market researchers label us anyway, mostly as particular types of consumers, which the dictionary, by the way, describes as "destroying, squandering, using up." Whatever we are, we are constantly communicating, by email, on the phone, being paged or paging. We work fifty hours a week mostly, both of us, if there are two adults sharing a home, and relegate much of the raising of our children to day-care centers and schools. We don't have time to play, to love, to care. Stopping to help a stranger is out of the question, Good Samaritan laws notwithstanding.

And then we don't understand why our kids use drugs, become addicted to computers, and chew with their mouths open. We are down to one, maybe two, good friends, and panic when we discover a pocket of uncommitted time in our days. Surely it is because we've forgotten to write down something that needs doing. We're burdened with duties, cramming more and more into our days, wondering what we're doing wrong. At the rate we're going, by the year 2053 we'll have lost all of our social skills, if we haven't all died of sleep deprivation.

Come to think of it, the fatigue alone just might do us in. "The cost of fatigue for the 25 million people who work at night or on rotating shifts is estimated to be $77 billion. When you add in the remainder of the workforce, the cost of fatigue is estimated to be well over $150 billion: the result of slower job performance, poor-quality work, poor decision making, industrial accidents, and health-care claims. And drowsy drivers are believed to be the number one cause of fatal single-car accidents." (Ed Coburn, letter to the editor, *Inc. Technology*, No. 2, June 15, 1998, p.15)

Somewhere in there our yearning for an authentic life has translated into believing that authenticity is equated to higher standards of living. Bah, humbug, I say. Was it Marx who said that wars are caused by such excessive wants? I vaguely recall him writing somewhere that the only reason you and I pursue money is to satisfy undisciplined bodily needs. Plato held this opinion as well. And money in the form of an ever higher standard of living is most of the problem. All this stuff is making us nuts. And miserable.

In a recent meditation class, students complained that they could not find even five minutes in their days to sit quietly. They had too many demands on their time, they said: phone calls to return, emails to check, books to finish, families to feed. Their lives had become a series of beeps and rings: telephones ringing, the microwave beeping that something was cooked, watches beeping as a reminder that a child needed picking up or a pill needed to be taken, computers dinging that a new email message had arrived.

How do we stop before we all die of heart failure? First, by remembering that we were pretty happy before all this hyperactivity and sleep deprivation took over. When I grew up we had one radio, one telephone, and one television. It was enough. One television meant the family spent time together, even if it was only to watch *Lassie*. One radio meant that we learned to depend on my parents to tell us whether or not school was closed because of weather. One telephone meant that we took turns and learned not to spend more than five minutes or so on a call. As a result, whole days were not lost to hypercommunication. These days, I have multiples of all three—televisions, radios, telephones. So does everyone I know. Plus most of my colleagues in the work world have pagers and faxes and computers and cell phones. It never occurs to us, as we build up these collections of "time savers," that each time we buy something it could take more time from us in the form of set-up time, maintenance, and repair. And that doesn't even count the time we spend using them all. It didn't used to be like this. The cost in lost personal time is tremendous.

We need to remember back when we weren't so overwhelmingly burdened so we can recognize when we aren't. Happily there are also trailblazers who can show us how to rewind to where our daily focus is on what really matters to us—relationships, spirituality, a life well lived. Joe Dominguez and Vicki Robin are two of the wisest trailblazers around. The authors of *Your Money or Your Life,* Joe and Vicki have accumulated massive amounts of research showing that people in this society are the same amount of happy whether their income is under $1,000 a month or over $4,000. Further, contrary to what we might expect, a study of a thousand lottery winners over a ten-year period discovered that very few of them felt happier as a result of their increased income. Meanwhile, we try to find happiness by increasing our wealth so we can have more things, more experiences, safer houses, security in our old age. All this in spite of the fact that one juicy economic depression could put us all out on the streets. Our increasingly affluent lifestyles continue to deplete the earth, clog our arteries, pollute the air, water, and soil, and still we yearn for wealth. Still we take on added duties and obligations because surely they'll get us to where we want to be.

Our lives are too cluttered. So cluttered that we don't even notice the mountain cabin with a welcome sign on its door because we're driving by too fast, talking on our cell phone.

Dominguez and Robin offer guidelines for a different lifestyle that would allow for retreats, for breaks from all the stuff, the beeps, the obligations. Here are their ground rules for living:

1. Save money by not trying to impress other people.

2. Don't go shopping.

3. Live within your means.

4. Take care of what you have.

5. Wear it out.

6. Do it yourself.

7. Anticipate your needs to eliminate impulse buying.

8. Before buying anything, research its quality, value, durability, and potential uses.

9. Get it for less.

10. Buy it used.

(Joe Dominguez and Vicki Robin, *Your Money or Your Life: Transforming Your Relationship with Money and Achieving Financial Independence,* New York: Viking Penguin, 1993)

I can remember first seeing the ground rules and saying to myself, "not bloody likely" (a leftover expression from my Australian boarding school years). But then I thought about them one weekend while I was on a retreat and trying not to think at all. The first round of insight had to do with debt and realizing that the more debt I have the more burdened I feel. I then thought about how Buddha taught that we have to take responsibility for our own lives and that, no matter who we are, someone else will always be criticizing us. So trying to impress anybody with material possessions is a useless exercise at best. I realized how much time and money I could save if I let go of trying to have updated furniture, the newest hairstyle, fashion princess shoes.

Since I had a whole weekend, I kept going. Eventually I realized that I really only need about half of what I thought I needed to live on. If I were choosier with clients, I would need less income and I could stay closer to home. I later discovered that socially conscious companies tend to have casual clothing days as a company norm. Needing only casual clothes and fewer miles driven meant that I would have more time to take care of what I have, like my car, which continues to purr at 144,000 miles. I would have time to plan for purchases and shop for lower prices for the few things I really need, and to go pick my own fruits and vegetables.

If you are over forty-five years old, you have less than 280,000 hours left in your life. Perhaps you have noticed that they are flying past. Do you want to spend them living or dying? Decide what really matters to you.

Look around. What you have is enough. In fact, maybe it's too much. This could be just the day to make yourself a sign that "enough is enough," and pledge to live by it. When one of my best friends first made the same suggestion to me, I thought he was joking, but I made the sign anyway, since he's my friend.

It really put a spotlight on my own greediness, and reminded me that I didn't need to bring more stuff into my little apartment without getting rid of something. It forced me to admit that I shop for clothes whenever I am utterly confused by an intimate relationship and in need of distraction. The sign has saved me thousands of dollars in new car costs, and reminded me that my jeans are just fine and that, at my age, new ones won't make me look like the girls in the TV commercials. If I ever break down and get a tattoo, it will be those three words: Enough is enough. They've taught me more than any other saying that has graced my refrigerator door.

To find out what really matters to you, give yourself the gift of some solitude. It is the only thing that gives us the space we need to honestly look at ourselves and our lives to determine if we are headed where we want to be headed or if we are drowning in samsara. As a child, Buddha sat in solitude. As a young man, he sat. When he was trying to decide whether to leave his life as a prince, with all its seductions, he would go off to be alone when everyone else was asleep. He even left his spiritual teachers and five best friends to be alone. The solitude gave him the time and space he needed to break through delusion and eventually realize his own enlightenment.

Every time I follow the Buddha's lead, my life changes dramatically. I always end up coming home and clearing out my calendar so there is more free space, more playtime. I reconfigure my days so there is more time for meditation or contemplation and to do the simple chores of cleaning, mending, and cooking. The things that need to be dropped leap off of the pages of my "to do" lists: all the business lunches and breakfasts I've agreed to, the social events with almost strangers whose values are so different from my own, and definitely the cocktail parties— I have no dresses.

When I follow the Buddha's example, I remember that being compassionate includes setting limits, like just saying no. Although it seems like a contradiction, saying no is actually an act of compassion for others, because when we do things that aren't appropriate or we're just too damn tired to fully participate in, they only get a piece of us—a small, crabby piece, if you are anything like me. And it shows compassion for ourselves, a reminder that we're just as precious as everyone else and sometimes we need to be nurtured as well.

It is in solitude that we rediscover gratitude for the people in our lives—our children, our teachers, our lovers. I, for one, make vows to be more attentive, more respectful, more openly appreciative.

There is work to be done. Find your mountain and your cabin before it is too late, before you've drowned in the hell realm of an overburdened life, before you've been abandoned by all of those now dear to you, so you can spend some time sorting through your life to discover the things that truly matter. If you don't have your own mountain, I offer you mine. It is Dechen Choling in East Meredith, New York. These days the telephone number is 607-278-5144. For $9 a day and some manual labor, you can have a hundred and thirty acres of the Catskills to your-self—for looking deeply at your life and to give you the courage to make the changes your heart wants you to make.

Ask for cabin number three.

꙳

Chapter Four

Getting to Peaceful and Calm

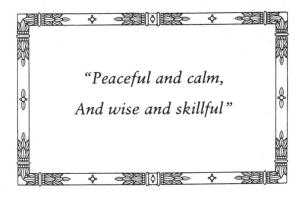

> *"Peaceful and calm,*
> *And wise and skillful"*

The characteristics of a psychopathic personality:

1. ***Superficial charm*** "The typical psychopath will seem particularly agreeable and make a distinctly positive impression when he is first encountered. Alert and friendly in his attitude, he is easy to talk with and seems to have a good many genuine interests....(Even so) the psychopath cannot be depended upon to show the ordinary responsiveness to special consideration or kindness or trust."

2. ***Intelligence*** "Psychometric tests also very frequently show him of superior intelligence...more than the average person, he is likely to seem free from social or emotional impediments, from the minor distortions, peculiarities, and awkwardnesses so common among the successful."

3. ***An absence of delusions or other signs of irrational thinking*** "He does not hear voices. Genuine delusion cannot be demonstrated. There is no valid depression, consistent pathologic elevation of mood, or irresistible pressure of activity. Excellent logical reasoning is maintained."

4. ***An absence of nervousness*** "The psychopath is nearly always free from minor reactions popularly regarded as neurotic or as constituting nervousness....It is highly typical for him not only to escape the abnormal anxiety and tension fundamentally characteristic of this whole diagnostic group but also show a relative immunity from such anxiety and worry that might be judged normal."

5. ***Unreliable*** "On many occasions he shows no sense of responsibility whatsoever....No matter how binding the obligation, how urgent the circumstances, how important the matter, this holds true. Furthermore the question of whether or not he is to be confronted with his failure or his disloyalty and called to account for it appears to have little effect on his attitude."

6. ***Untruthfulness and insincerity*** "The psychopath shows a remarkable disregard for the truth....Typically he is at ease and unpretentious in making a serious promise or in (falsely) exculpating himself from accusations, whether grave or trivial....Candor and trustworthiness seem implicit in him...he will lie about any matter, under any circumstances, and often for no good reason."

7. ***Lack of remorse or shame*** "The psychopath apparently cannot accept substantial blame for the various misfortunes which befall him and which he brings down upon others. Usually he denies emphatically all responsibility and directly accuses others as responsible...he does not show the slightest evidence of major humiliation or regret."

8. ***A lack of conscience*** "Not only is the psychopath undependable, but also in more active ways he cheats, deserts, annoys, brawls, fails, and lies without any apparent compunction....He will commit

theft, forgery, adultery, fraud, and other deeds for astonishingly small stakes...."

9. **A failure to learn from experience** "He throws away excellent opportunities to make money, to achieve a rapprochement with his wife, to be dismissed from the hospital, or to gain other ends that he sometimes spent considerable effort toward gaining."

10. **An incapacity for love** "The psychopath is always distinguished by egocentricity. (He) seldom shows anything that, if the chief facts were known, would pass even in the eyes of lay observers as love....Connected with this is an inability to really feel strong emotions. (His) is an emotional poverty."

11. **A lack of insight** "He has absolutely no capacity to see himself as others see him....Usually instead of facing facts that would ordinarily lead to insight, he projects, blaming his troubles on others with the flimsiest of pretext but with elaborate and subtle realization."

12. **Fatalistic and uninviting behavior with drink and sometimes without** "Although some psychopaths do not drink at all and others drink rarely, considerable overindulgence in alcohol is very often prominent in the life story....A peculiar sort of vulgarity, domineering rudeness, petty bickering or buffoonish quasi-maulings of wife, mistress, or children, and quick shifts between maudlin and vainglorious moods, although sometimes found in ordinary alcoholics...are pathognomonic of the psychopath and in him alone reach full and precocious flower....Alcohol, as a sort of catalyst, sometimes contributes a good deal to the long and varied series of outlandish pranks and inanely coarse scenes...."

(Hervey Cleckley, M.D., *The Mask of Sanity: An Attempt to Clarify Some Issues About the So Called Psychopathic Personality*, 5th ed., Augusta, Ga.: Emily S. Cleckley, 1987; reprinted with the generous permission of Emily S. Cleckley)

For most of my adult life I figured my father was simply an alcoholic, womanizing workaholic who just happened to be wildly successful in corporate America. Then my mother decided, after I had been ordained for a couple of years, to tell me the details of the rest of the story. It turns out that he is also a psychopath. She figured this out when my siblings and I were much younger, but didn't want to say anything for fear of upsetting us. Here's the story she told me to break the news: When I was a tiny baby my parents and I lived in Lafayette, Indiana. My father, twenty-one, was an engineering student at Purdue. My mother, just sixteen, basically spent her days taking care of me in a tiny married student apartment, with occasional breaks to play baseball in the streets with the other neighborhood kids.

My father was rarely around because he was working at the railroad when he wasn't going to classes or parties without my mother. When I was about eight months old, my mother started getting evening phone calls from someone who threatened to kill me. The terrifying thing was that the person would sometimes describe the clothes I had worn that day. My mother kept the phone calls to herself, not even telling my father. She figured that she would watch the neighborhood, and me, very carefully until she figured out who it was. Then she would tell my father and go to the police.

The phone calls increased in frequency over several months. Finally one night the caller told her he would kill me that night and went on to describe the pajamas I was wearing. Terrified, my mother grabbed me and locked us both in the bathroom. We were found the next morning by university officials concerned neighbors had contacted because they had heard my screaming through the night. My mother, who had jammed her body between me and the door, was frozen in fear. I was in the bathtub. To this day she doesn't remember the next six months.

Twenty-five years later my father casually admitted to her that he had been the caller. He thought it was pretty funny.

When she told me this story, other memories of my father came to me. His lack of affection for us; the lewd drunkenness; regularly being thrown out of his apartment after my mother divorced him; his cruelties to his later wives; and clues to other corrupt behavior—worse ones.

36

But the worst part was seeing my own pattern, and those of my sisters, of falling in love with similar personality types, until I realized that I could add up a soccer team's worth of psychopaths we had all tried to love.

At first, some part of me wanted to wallow in the tragedy of it all, to feel perpetually sorry for all of us, and to wail for the pain of my mother's life. Most of me, though, reacted with a deep compassion for both my parents, for all of my siblings, and for myself. At about the same time my mother told me this story, a few people close to me started sharing similar life histories—deeply painful stories of horrific physical and psychological abuse, from alcoholism to sexual abuse to flat-out abandonment. One friend told me about how, at age three, she had saved her mother's life as her father was beating her to death. She climbed up on the kitchen counter, picked up a phone, and called an operator to say she needed help for her mommy who was hurting. The ambulance just made it in time.

Another friend, a much loved and respected dean of a university, casually mentioned the consistent sexual abuse he had lived with as a child, while we were waiting to be served lunch at a local restaurant. And another friend told me about how her former husband had sexually abused their son when he was a baby and how it took her years to get help from the courts. After hearing her story, I understood how a parent could kill to protect her child.

We are surrounded by and subject to the worst behavior imaginable. Most of us have been touched by it by now. Beyond social activism and working for institutional and cultural reforms to address such tragic behavior, what can we do? What would Buddha do?

His answer is clear. Once we're out of physical danger, have done whatever we can to put an end to abusive behavior, and have had some time to mourn whatever we've lost, let it go. Just let it go. Stop thinking about it. Stop obsessing. It's past and all we really have is right now. The story that best demonstrates this teaching is one in which a king whines to Buddha about how difficult his life is...so full of suffering, of things going wrong, never the way he planned. He is so worried and so upset. Can Buddha help?

The response? "Pull the arrow right out." "What arrow?" The Buddha replied: "If you are shot by an arrow, and the only way to live is to pull the arrow out, would it make any sense to obsess about how the arrow got there, or who shot it, or why he or she shot it? By the time you got all the answers you would be dead. Just pull the arrow out."

It sounds harsh, but it works. We need to pull the arrow of pain right out of our hearts and move on. Pain, suffering, difficulty, and tragedy are bound to hit each of us sooner or later. And it will make us crazy for a while. Then we'll mourn, but then we need to move on, because staying in the past stalls spiritual progress.

We need to decide to change our minds. That is all and that is everything. We need to see the tragedy as a lesson hard won, as a window to the deepest wisdom possible, and then move on. Our obsessing about incidents long after they are over keeps us miserable—the blaming, the whining, the need to be the holiest and most long-suffering of martyrs. My father's behavior to my mother, myself, and my sisters is, mercifully, past. To obsess about it now wastes the precious moments of whatever life we have left.

Replacing the pain with spiritual practice fills the hole in our broken hearts with compassion and empathy, which will, I promise, eventually shift to peace and calm. Like Aladdin's magic carpet, spiritual practice can pull us out from under the mind demons that haunt us and fly us to where we can take refuge in Buddha, *dharma* (the teachings of Buddhism), and *sangha* (community). Practice gives me the strength to change my mind about a situation so I can let go and move on. I trust it to give me the courage that brings peace. As you test my words out you'll see how changing your mind, even about seemingly small things, can shift your whole life experience.

At our most recent Buddha's Birthday celebration it was my job to hand out the word sheet for the Great Compassion Dharani, one of the chants we regularly sing at the Ann Arbor Zen Buddhist Temple. Actually, the sheet doesn't even have words on it, just sounds. Here are the first few lines:

Sin myo jang gu Tae da ra ni
Na mo ra da na da ra ya ya
Na mag al yak pa ro gi je se ba ra ya
Mo ji sa da ba ya
Ma ha sa da ba ya
Ma ha ga ro ni ga ya

In the ritual associated with the chanting, the person handing out the sheets hands it with both hands to the person who is receiving it, also with both hands. We then make a deep bow to each other. On that day, as official sheet-hander-outer, I had given out all the sheets but two or three. At the back of the meditation hall, sitting in a chair was one of our older members, a woman who has seen me through many of the peaks and valleys—mostly valleys—of my adult life. When I went to hand her a sheet, she frowned and said, "No. I hate it."

I grinned, remembering that I had hated it as well. For a long time. It had no English translation, so it was impossible to understand. I wonder what changed, because now I love it. Now it's my *Ally McBeal* song, the song I instantly thought of when Ally's psychiatrist, played by Tracey Ullman, told her that she needed a song to give her courage and fill her with good energy. (And yes, I'll admit it here: "It's Raining Men" was a close second for me. Karmic habits die hard.) Anyway, that chant is the song in my head when I am at my happiest. Actually, it's there almost all the time. If I am lucky it will be the last sound I hear as I die.

How did the shift happen? The moment I decided to love it. Just like that. I pulled the arrow right out, saying to myself, "This is a part of your chosen path. Embracing it beats fighting it." And so it has.

Changing our minds changes our worlds. My daughter's father has been one of the most difficult people in my life. He yells so hard that it's scary. The years I spent with him were both wonderful and horrible. When we parted ways we were both enraged with each other. It was a rage that lasted for years, even though we both worked hard, through a joint custody arrangement, to raise our daughter skillfully.

When she and I lived at the Zen Buddhist temple, her father would occasionally do or say something that would set me off on a rant for days. One time it was over Christmas plans. After a particularly excruciating phone call, I went downstairs to the kitchen, where Haju, the temple priest, was making pecan pies. Pacing furiously, I complained about the man in all the ways I knew how, berating myself for having had the miserable karma that had led me to him in the first place. (No, he is not a psychopath. Those relationships came later.)

Haju listened quietly until I was all done, and then she handed me one of the pecan pies she had baked and said, "When you go over to his house to pick Jamie up, maybe you can give him this." Stunned, I started to laugh, suddenly realizing that all of my suffering was self-induced. He was just being him. I was the one stacking the behavior with values and judgments and "how could he's." At once our relationship started to shift.

The next time Jamie called me in tears from his house after they had had a father–teenage girl argument, I decided right then and there to think of him as my best friend, as someone who was honestly struggling to raise a daughter well in chaotic times. Instead of my usual ranting and threatening, I went to see him. I sat on his porch with him and shared my own frustrations with raising a sensitive kid. He smiled sympathetically when I told him how I had bought the local bookstore out of all their raising-teenage-girl books one Monday morning, after a particularly exhausting weekend. He told me about how rude and uncommunicative she was, about her arrogant attitude. I told him about some of the painful things that had happened to her that week: the cruel teasings of an ex-boyfriend, malicious gossip that had been spread at school, the lunchroom tantrum of her best friend.

He thanked me. I offered to lend the books to him. He offered to pay for a trip to Oregon so I could see a close friend. And I've begun to hear comments at home about how he has changed, how fun it is to do things with him. I'm glad, since he's my best friend.

Carolyn Myss, a well-known and respected intuitive healer, talks about letting go in the context of disease. When we stop clinging to our suffering, when we stop identifying with it, it can go away. When we think of ourselves as healthy, as wholesome, we are.

When Ron walks past people in Ann Arbor, people tend to avert their eyes. He is skeleton thin and walks with a huge limp that is the result of breaking his back in a diving accident as a child. His enormous dark eyes pierce you when they look at you, and sometimes when I see him his skin is so pale that I wonder if he is dying. I've been thinking that for years now. More than fifteen. In that period Ron *has* almost died, been in the hospital, and suffered some serious physical ailments. Even so, if you asked him about his health, he would grin ear to ear and say, "Excellent." The energy in his voice would tell you that it is true. There is simply no clinging to any thoughts of disease. Instead, every day is healthy and wholesome, and that is all there is to that. The man will outlive all of us.

So. What if you aren't lucky enough to have a psychopathic parent to motivate you to change your thinking? Happily psychopathic bosses and partners are almost as effective, and there seem to be quite a few populating the country these days. Once you've had some exposure to such types and managed to get yourself out from under their spell—and I say, do whatever you have to to put time and distance between you— you can practice pulling the arrows out. By simply deciding to let go. The space that is freed up can then be filled with the peace and calm you've been looking for. They've been there all this time in the shadow of your own ego needs. They just needed someone to agitate you enough to find them again.

Chapter Five

Nasty People as Secret Bodhisattvas

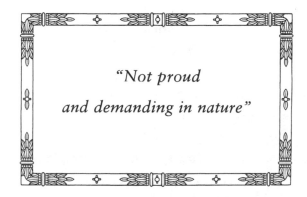

"Not proud and demanding in nature"

Once a week we make this Bodhisattva vow at the temple: "Thus by the virtue collected through all that I have done may the pain of every living creature be completely cleared away." And sometimes there is this little crabby voice in my head that adds, "Except Jodie Watson!"

Jodie Watson is a nasty person with whom I work. She's the kind of nasty that turns away from me when I say good morning in my most cheerful voice. And then she literally moves her chair away from me. If I ask her to do something, her way of acknowledging me is to look up and say, with deep exasperation, "What do you want?" Whatever my answer is, her usual response is, "I don't have time." So I've learned not to ask.

And heaven help me if I make a mistake like a typo. She stands up in the open office space and says, loudly enough so most people on the floor can hear her, "What have you done now?!" Every time.

Perhaps you have your own Jodie. For a long time I was happy to recite the Bodhisattva vow as long as I could throw in the "except for Jodie" part and add another name or two when I was in a really cranky mood. My own proud and demanding nature was properly appalled by her refusal to live by my expectation of what a good administrative assistant should be. She rubbed me raw, that woman.

For a while I halfheartedly made excuses for her behavior: We're all sleep deprived; we're all trying to do the work of two or three people. But then my brain answered back, "Forget that. We're all supposed to be in this together. The woman is a first-class bitch." Twenty years ago, I probably would have come home on the toughest days, stuck some pins in a doll, and called it quits. But that was pre-seminary.

So I was stuck. The Metta Sutra says we should cherish all beings. The four great vows we chant at almost every temple service promise to liberate *all others*. My friend Kodu told me that once upon a time there was a sutra that said you could leave some people out. Like Hitler, pedophiles, abusive mates or parents, and corrupt cops. I spent a month looking for the ancient teaching, desperate to find an escape clause. Nothing. Instead, over and over, the sutras teach that all things are precious. *All things. All people. No exceptions.*

At one point I thought I had found something in the last book of the Avatamsaka Sutra. The main character is a young pilgrim named Sudhana, who visits over fifty different teachers asking them for the rules of the spiritual road. Somewhere in the middle he visits this spunky woman, Asha, who is known for her bluntness and realistic take on life.

Sudhana asks her what the real deal is; what do enlightening beings (that's us) really need to practice? I held my breath, reading the passage. Here's what Asha replies: "(Enlightening beings) free all sentient beings from the sicknesses of afflictions, (they) are like the sun because they eliminate the darkness of ignorance of all sentient beings, (their) minds are like the earth because they are a refuge for all sentient beings, (they) are like air because they benefit all sentient beings, (they) are like lamps producing the light of knowledge for all sentient beings, (they) are like clouds raining truth with a quiet sound, (they) are like the moon because they radiate a web of light beams of virtue." (*Entry into the Realm of Reality*, translated by Thomas Cleary, Boston: Shambhala Publications, 1989, p. 89) I was doomed. No way out. No exceptions. Jodie counts. What to do?

I looked for teachers that could help. Happily, they showed themselves almost immediately. My first lesson happened at a lunch with a monk named Hui-min, who, last I heard, was an abbot in one of Taiwan's large monasteries. He is a young, handsome man who radiates warmth and humor. He is childlike and adorably smart. Hui-min used to come to Ann Arbor periodically to visit with a Chinese sangha. I was lucky enough to be included in one of their luncheons for him at a local restaurant. It was a great honor since the lunches appeared to be limited to a handful of people. I asked if I could bring my partner so he could see what a real Zen master was like. He didn't know much about Buddhism, and frankly had a harsh streak in him that I hoped could be mellowed by spending some time with Hui-min.

We went to the lunch. My partner immediately took hold of the conversation and wouldn't let go. He started out by listing examples of the corruptions we all live with, and then moved on to the conspiracies of all governments, and then argued for total population control, including the genetic screening of fetuses. I sat there listening for as long as I could (about twenty minutes) and finally, embarrassed and frustrated, turned to Hui-min. "How do you deal with negative people?" I asked him. His answer? A huge, happy grin. "Why, I learn so much from them. Don't you?" He was loving every minute of our lunch and clearly enjoyed and liked my friend. I was stunned and confused.

Then it happened again. This time I was with Sunim, my teacher. A few of us were sitting around the eating table in the Ann Arbor temple late one hot evening. Sunim and an attendant, a young Canadian

45

monk, had just arrived from Toronto almost ten hours later than expected. Sunim sat eating ice cream while the young man explained their tardiness.

It turned out that the border guard had decided, for some reason, that he didn't like the looks of Sunim. First he made the two unload everything in their car. Then he searched it, inch by inch. They were instructed to sit in an office for hours while he went through their papers. When he found that they were in order, he started to interrogate Sunim, insulting him and making racial comments.

As I listened, I got angrier and angrier until I looked over at Sunim, who was calmly eating his ice cream, his face expressionless. No anger. No ill will. Unbelievable. I figured he must be too exhausted to be angry anymore. Ever the eager student, I asked him, "Sunim, what do you think of this situation?" His eyes lit up and he grinned like the Cheshire cat. "Oh, that guy," he said. "That guy is a good friend."

What?!

And then I saw the wisdom of Sunim's reaction. He let the guard just be who he was without any reaction. As a result, when Sunim was allowed, finally, to cross the border, the entire incident was done—an entertaining day that was finished. Since then, the same fellow has waved Sunim across the border.

If Sunim can, we can. I decided to try out what I called "the Sunim take" with Jodie. While not exactly pain free, it has certainly been an education. I began driving to the office saying to myself, "Every situation is simply a mirror of ourselves. And everything we think or do in a situation tells us exactly what we need to know about ourselves." Over and over I would say these words as I walked in the door and over to Jodie's desk to let her know I had arrived for a meeting.

Her behavior, which never wavered, was a perfect mirror. I could tell exactly how strong my practice was within seconds of saying good morning. On days where I got a kick out of her grouchiness, my practice was strong. It meant I had taken time to meditate for an hour before driving to work and I had had a good night's sleep. When my reaction to her behavior was irritation, it usually meant I had done prostrations but had only made time for ten minutes of sitting, or I hadn't had enough sleep. On the days when my reaction was righteous anger, I realized that I had rushed through early morning practice, failing to do more than a few prostrations and only a little chanting. My negative reactions were strongest when I had been greedy the day before, staying up into the wee hours of the night because I wanted to read or talk on the telephone with friends, or watch a late-night basketball game. I saw my own "proud and demanding" nature and how it popped up every time I walked through her door. I wanted that woman to be Saint Jodie. I wanted her to be what I wanted, rather than who she was.

I also learned about persistence, and how I really needed to stick with my practice and to dig deeper if I was going to be able to honestly feel any friendliness toward her. In fact, persistence became a core component of my spiritual work. I remembered an editorial I had cut out of *Elle* magazine about the importance of just continuing the work at hand, in spite of tough obstacles:

> Describing his many years of dealing with skeptical colleagues and disdainful grant review committees, Dr. Folkman (a recipient of the Breast Cancer Research Foundation's Jill Rose Award) posed the question anyone who has tried to make a difference comes up against: "How does one know when to keep going and when to cut one's losses and start a new project?... I learned that sometimes in research, as in other...activities, you just have to keep going even when you are not at all sure that you will find something important at the end of the road." He went on to quote a wonderful description by E. L. Doctorow *(Ragtime, Billy Bathgate)* of what it's like to write a book: "Writing is like driving at night. You cannot see beyond your headlights...but you can make the whole trip that way!"
>
> (Editor's page, *Elle*, January 1998, p. 24)

For several weeks, I had that editorial taped onto my bedroom door as a reminder that the point of spiritual practice is to just do it, and that the Jodies of the world are simply reminders that practice does have an impact on our lives. Perseverance. I vowed it knowing that it was my means to a heartfelt Bodhisattva vow.

As soon as I started to see the pattern of my reactions, I began to use Jodie's behavior as a teaching tool, and actually started to look forward to seeing her because it meant that I would get immediate feedback on how I was doing. Although she wasn't quite as powerful a teacher as Sunim has been, she was a close second.

As I used her behavior to reflect my own spiritual standing, I started to discover things about her I had never known or realized before. For instance, she had gained more than twenty pounds in the year I was working with her. She was also wheezing a lot, and I noticed that her hands were arthritic and that she often wore wrist braces. During that time she was getting daily personal phone calls about her sister, who was suffering from Alzheimer's disease. Her sister needed to be institutionalized and Jodie was her only living relative.

The more I learned about her, the more my compassion for her grew. At times it became really hard not to cry for the pain and sadness of her life. She reminded me again and again that Buddha's admonition to be grateful for everything is a literal truth. Learning people's stories helps us to be grateful for everything and everyone. So much is explained there. In *Finding Freedom: Writings from Death Row*, Jarvis Jay Masters writes about the day he learned the stories of some of the men with whom he shared his time. On that day he suddenly noticed how scarred the bodies of the men in San Quentin were. Standing beside a fence in the exercise yard, he found himself staring at three of the inmates. Whiplike scars covered their bodies. There were scars behind their legs, on their backs, and across their ribs. One of them, John, even had scars all over his face. When Jarvis asked him about them, John replied that "his father had loved him enough to teach him how to fight when he was only five years old. He learned from the beatings he got....

He pointed to a nasty scar on his upper shoulder. Laughing, he told us that his father had hit him with a steel rod when John tried to protect his mother from being beaten." (Jarvis Jay Masters, *Finding Freedom: Writings from Death Row*, Junction City, Calif.: Padma Publishing, 1997, p. 68)

Jarvis's story is as wrenching: "That day I spoke openly to my friends about my physical and mental abuse as a child. I told them I had been neglected and then abandoned by my parents, heroin addicts, when I was very young. I was beaten and whipped by my stepfather. My mother left me and my sisters alone for days with our newborn twin brother and sister when I was only four years old. The baby boy died a crib death and I always believed it was my fault, since I had been made responsible for him. I spoke to them of the pain I had carried through more than a dozen institutions, pain I could never face. And I explained how all of these events ultimately trapped me in a pattern of lashing out against everything." (*Finding Freedom*, p. 71)

How many children do we lose to death row because we don't pay attention to their stories? How many Jodies do we leave out of our vows because we don't try to understand them?

My daughter Jamie gave me the last piece of the puzzle I needed to be able to make the Bodhisattva vow with a full heart. I had forgotten but have recently rediscovered that teenage girls can become dangerously difficult when their hormones kick into overdrive. The first person they often turn on in their insta-rage is a best friend. Jamie has several friends who turn on her fairly regularly. My guess is that she returns the compliment…it's just that I don't hear about that side of the equation too often.

One of her friends is so skilled at becoming enraged that about once a year I'll get a phone call from Jamie begging me, between sobs, to come and get her because of something her friend has said or done. I don't, because life can be rough and tumbly, and surviving such situations will build her capacity for coping with her self-prophesied future as a writer for *Vanity Fair*. On the other hand, as the one on the other end of the hysterical phone calls, I admit that I usually wish that her good friend would either grow up or move to another town—preferably before the weekend.

The last time I got a phone call, I was angry at Jamie's friend. She had belittled my precious daughter in front of a large group of their closest buddies. Jamie called me at lunch to plead with me to drive her home. I declined, reminding her that she was bigger than the situation. I told her that I would, however, get to school a little early at the end of the day so she would have a solid stress break before swim practice that night.

When I got to the school, there was Jamie standing next to the same friend who had caused the sobs three short hours ago. Jamie asked if we could give her a ride home. I nodded yes, afraid of what might pop out of my mouth if I started to say anything. And on top of that, Jamie was utterly sweet to the girl all the way to her house, which just happened to be on the other side of the city. She complimented her on her accent in their foreign language class and said she wished she could understand geometry as quickly. She mentioned that one of the cute boys from the lacrosse team had asked about her and, when we got to the girl's house, smiled and said, "I'll see you tomorrow," with only friendliness in her voice.

I was amazed. And I admit it, irritated. I ordered Jamie to sit in the front seat next to me on our way home so I could lecture her on not rewarding negative behavior. Just as I was about to open my mouth, some wiser part of me first asked her, "Why were you so nice?" Jamie proceeded to tell me a little of the girl's story: that her parents had no time for her, that her big brother was facing a jail sentence for breaking and entering, that her boyfriend had just dumped her. Nobody in her life was kind to her. "Mom, someone has to teach her the behavior." Out of the mouths of babes.

Jamie was right. I decided to try her strategy out on Jodie, treating her as a delicate friend. I brought her information about Alzheimer's I had found on the Net and asked her opinion of dating younger men. She said, do it because they keep you young: "Better yet, as long as he's over twenty-one, the law's on your side, honey!" And, do you know, she actually smiled when she said it. I bought extra bagels at Zingerman's so I could bring her one when I was in her building, and told her about the book my mother is writing that tells *all* the family secrets. "Like you don't," she said. We went out to lunch together. I'm watching for tickets to *Jesus Christ Superstar* because I think she'd really love it.

Of course, there's a downside to all this. Since Jodie isn't nasty anymore, I can't quite tell how my practice is going. But I'm keeping my eye out for someone else who can make me crazy. Happily there's a man at the local grocery store who will probably work out just fine. In the twenty years I've lived in Ann Arbor, he's never once said good morning to me, never once said thank you for shopping at his store. I'll have to go there more often.

Thank Buddha for difficult people, for they can bring us to our emotional knees. They are the bodhisattvas you and I need to see how strong our spiritual practice really is. As long as we are surrounded by Buddhas who insist on being peaceful and calm and wise and skillful all the time, we'll never know what work is left to be done. Give me someone cutting me off on a highway any day.

Postscript:

What if someone is so nasty, so abusive, that you literally lie awake at night not knowing what to do or where to turn? Then, remember Vamsa. Vamsa was the only kingdom where Buddha struck out 2,500 years ago. He was good friends with the other three kings of his day. But Vamsa? Not only did the king refuse to feed any of Buddha's monks, he ordered his subjects to cover their wells with straw so they couldn't even get any water to drink. If a monk was visibly dehydrated from thirst, a resident could give him alcohol.

When Buddha kept hearing reports from Vamsa of his followers getting drunk and doing stupid things, he went to see what was going on for himself. When he saw how the monks were treated, he went to see the king, who proceeded to kick him right out of the kingdom. When Buddha's followers asked him what he would do to help the king and his kingdom so they could grow spiritually, his response was dead silence. And he never returned to Vamsa.

What are the signs that your workplace, or a relationship, is so toxic that you've landed in Vamsa at the turn of this century? First, if there is clear and regular harassment of any kind: Vamsa. If you are in physical danger: Vamsa. If you are so distracted by someone's nastiness that you simply cannot get a grip on your spiritual practice: Vamsa. If I am in a situation and I am not sure it is Vamsa, I give it a thirty-day test (as long as I know I'm physically safe). If at the end of each day I say to myself, "It's Vamsa," I leave. It is not our job to support the functioning of utterly toxic environments. And it is not our job to help someone with an unrelenting nasty streak to create any more negative karma than he or she already has. For example, if my practice had suffered because of Jodie, it would have been Vamsa. But she's strengthened it, and she's become kinder over time.

You decide. The only thing I know is this: If it is Vamsa, the best thing you can do is get on your pony and ride out of town. Life is short, and time is precious.

Chapter Six

The Movie That Is Our Life

> "Let them not do
> the slightest thing
> That the wise would later
> reprove"

I have breakfast or lunch with one of my favorite former bosses every couple of months. Each time he asks me to have sex with him. Sometimes he asks in the middle of the meal. Sometimes he waits until the end. He's married. He's also sexy. He's smart, endowed with one of the best senses of humor this side of the Rockies, has totally great houses in different parts of the country so he can be comfortable in any season, and drives my favorite car. Sex with him would be great. I know because we've always worked well together—it's that same wavelength thing. He knows me, the funny smart parts and the neurotic parts, and still thinks I'm sexy.

I say no each time. Part of it is that I am determined not to have an affair with a mated man, determined to live by the precept not to take what is not given. I think of his wife and how hurt she would be by this particular betrayal. My guess is that part of her suspects that we've had an affair for years, since we traveled together when I worked for him. I want to tell her to relax, she's safe, but then, I'm not too sure what his relationship is with his other former employees. Mostly, though, I say no because I honestly believe that when I die I'll get a private showing of the movie that has been my life, and if I did have sex with him, watching that part of the movie would make me throw up all over myself I would be so ashamed, and I don't want the humiliation. So I'll keep saying no for as long as it takes.

"Let them not do the slightest thing that the wise would later reprove," shouts the Metta Sutra. What will your life's movie say to you about how you have spent your time? It's worth taking a quiet afternoon to recount to yourself your own story in a deeply honest way, in an effort to see not just where you've been but where you're headed. There is an old Zen teaching about this: If you want to understand why your life is like it is right now, study your past. If you want to see what your future will be like, study your present. Where are the actions the wise would later reprove? We all have them. And in the spiritual practice realm, small slights can be deeply harmful. We aren't home free just because we haven't committed any felonies.

Every Sunday afternoon in our 5 P.M. service in Ann Arbor, sangha members reflect on this. We chant for a while to open our hearts and then pause for the following reflections:

Let us reflect upon ourselves
Let us reflect upon what we've done this week
If you feel you've done something harmful to others
Please reflect upon this deeply
And ask forgiveness
So that we may be able to go forward in promoting
*   peace and happiness for all beings.*

Let us reflect upon ourselves
Let us reflect upon what we've done this week
If you feel some people have done harmful things, if you feel pain
If you feel anger for this
I ask you to forgive them
They might have done so out of their ignorance.

Also
Others who may have done harm
They may have done so out of ignorance
Please forgive them
Please forgive them so we can go forward in promoting
  peace and happiness for all beings.

Such reflections keep us aware of our own behaviors and our particular karmic patterns of screwing up. I am forever regretting my flip mouth, my fast pace, and my impatience. Reflecting on all three helps me to pay special attention to situations in which I'm likely to go awry so I can do some preventive pausing.

What makes you cringe when you think about your life's movie? Have you stopped the behavior? Vowed to stop? Asked for help? Made amends? As an incentive to consider these questions, please remember that karma crosses lifetimes. My vote is that we each vow to brush ourselves off and vow to truly live by a set of principles that can protect us from our weak moments, even if we have to keep starting over each day. This is the path the wise applaud.

Buddhist precepts are a helpful starting place. If you haven't seen them before, or don't have them permanently engraved into your gray matter, here is a simple rendition:

1. Do not harm but cherish all life.

2. Do not take what is not given but respect the things of others.

3. Do not engage in sexual promiscuity but practice purity of mind and self-restraint.

4. Do not lie but speak the truth.

5. Do not partake in the production and transactions of firearms or chemical poisons which are injurious to public health and safety, nor of drugs and liquors which confuse or weaken the mind.

6. Do not waste but conserve energy and natural resources.

7. Do not harbor enmity against the wrongs of others but promote peace and justice through nonviolent means.

8. Do not cling to things that belong to you but practice generosity and the joy of sharing.

If it feels like cleaning up your movie will take a lot of hard work, please know that you are in good company, and that unskilled behavior is an ancient problem. In Buddha's time there was a seven-day festival, The Simpleton's Festival, when people used to smear their bodies with ashes and cow dung and wander about uttering all manner of coarse talk, showing no respect for anyone and insulting anyone within range. One time when Buddha and his monks were staying at Jetavana Monastery, hearing that such a festival was going on, they waited out the seven days in a park. When they finally went begging into the city of Savatthi, their benefactors complained bitterly about the festival. It was so awful, they told the monks. Did Buddha have any response?

He did. He talked about how easy it was to sink into such behavior. (The Simpleton's Festival was just one example.) The other extreme would protect us from all becoming simpletons. Paying attention to the spiritual teachings, we would know what to do: Foolish and undiscriminating people indulge in heedlessness. The wise cherish mindfulness as a great treasure. The wise pay attention to their lives so that they won't stumble, so that they won't forget that the whole point of our lives is to learn how to live. So the wise would never reprove our behavior.

This mindfulness is invaluable. Over the years, as I've paid better attention, I have started to see subtleties in my life I used to completely miss. Having been in management consultant trenches for almost twenty years now, I can usually pick up on destructive behavioral patterns on the part of chief executive officers pretty quickly—sometimes in minutes. Back in my less than mindful days, I would immediately whack whoever it was on the side of the head with my insights, figuring that such information would be readily valued and acted upon. "You aren't delegating any work of substance." Or "You delegate too much without enough instructions to follow through on tasks." Or "Your continuous absence has led to an insurrection in the making. You need to be here every day, starting tomorrow."

I was wrong. While the insights were usually accurate, my timing needed work. These days, paying better attention to moods and other factors, I work hard to wait to be asked, or ask for permission to talk about a particular topic instead of blithely hammering away. Mindfulness. The wisdom that grows out of its practice is enormous.

How can we remember this teaching so we will want to watch the movie of our lives? Amulets help a lot here, like beads you can wear on your wrist. I have some I wear for particularly stressful situations as a constant reminder to pay attention, to be mindful. Rosaries. Statues. Holy pictures. Notes to yourself hanging in conspicuous places. For Christmas this year I embroidered handkerchiefs with W.W.B.D. (What would Buddha do?) for my closest dharma family members to remind them of their own intrinsic Buddha wisdom every time they blow their noses.

One of them, a recovering road rager, taught me the value of amulets. He has the best one I've seen. This is a fellow who is renowned for his cursing ability when it comes to other drivers. It's almost funny to think of this, because if you met him what you would see is this quiet, smiling person, lithe and muscular, with a mostly shaven head and sparkling eyes. You would notice that he is always helpful, doing chores that nobody else even notices need to be done. But put him in a car and the world shifts. Or it did. Until he bought a plastic Buddha statue and superglued it onto his dashboard, making us all slightly safer around these parts.

And if the going gets particularly rough? When the weaker part of me starts nagging at the other part of me that one hot night of sex with my former boss will not land me in a hell realm? That we're only talking about a second or so in the life movie? What if I know nobody will ever know because everyone in Ann Arbor is out of town for Labor Day weekend except the two of us? How do I refrain from ever making that call? What can any of us do in those moments when we can feel ourselves sliding into a situation that we know in our heart of hearts will be a mistake?

Aha. This is the job of spiritual bodyguards. Maybe your spiritual bodyguard is a local monk or minister. Maybe it's a best friend who will tell you that what you are about to do is totally stupid. Maybe it's a saint—dead or alive. Mine is Tara, one of the Tibetan saints. Tara's title is "Mother of All the Buddhas," whose self-proclaimed job description reads: "I, O Lord, shall lead (beings) across the great flood of their diverse fears; therefore the eminent seers sing of me in the world by the name of Tara." (Martin Willson, *In Praise of Tara: Songs of the Saviouress*, rev. ed., Somerville, Mass.: Wisdom Publications, 1996) Part of her draw is that she is believed to offer worldly benefits, notably her ability to save you and me from major screw-ups and any fears that might be keeping us awake at night. You know, fear of lions, elephants, fire, snakes, robbers, imprisonment, and any man-eating demons. And if those aren't enough, there is always pride, delusion, anger, envy, wrong views, greed, attachment, and doubt, emotions that lead us directly into the screw-up realm.

Tara is also the Buddhist form of the great mother goddess, the feminine archetype embedded in the minds of all of us. In this role she is concerned with birth, death, peace, war, seasons, any form of life, and even the moon: "You should recognize all you see as Tara's body, all you hear as her divine speech, and all your thoughts as her divine wisdom. Every particle you eat is Tara, every molecule of air you breathe is her divine energy, the house you live in is her, when you lie down your head rests in her lap." *(In Praise of Tara)*

She has never, ever let me down when I have paused to ask her, "So, Tara, what would you say about this particular situation?" Sometimes I'll literally turn a painful experience over to Tara. "Tara, this one's for you." And those words are usually sufficient to set my deluded mind on pause until I can see a situation more clearly and find out the wise path. Find a bodyguard. Or two. So you can keep that movie's PG rating.

Here's a second method for staying on track. Think of the everyday heroes you know, the people who couldn't begin to understand why you would ever consider doing something the wise would reprove. Everyday heroes surround us. In my life, Robert Bartle plays that role for me. He is one of those people who periodically heads out of the country to help the people of some village who have no water. Or an organic farmer who needs someone to help with the planting. Robert heads out with a full heart. I have come to believe that his backpack is always packed. Or there's Jackie and Ann, who opened an organic bakery in the heart of one of Detroit's toughest neighborhoods, and if that wasn't enough, they recruit girls from an Alternatives for Girls program that has as its goal providing young women with an alternative living wage to prostitution.

On my bedroom wall I have a picture of three young women who are living on platforms high above the trees in the Canadian wilderness in an effort to focus the rest of the world's eyes on the environmental destruction that is taking place all around us. Beside that picture is one of a young girl who has chained herself to a logging machine. And in my journal I keep the story of Donna Parker and Anna Gerhardt. They are the two young women who entered Mitsubishi's Bank of California in San Francisco "dressed as girlfriends coming from the gym, their loose jackets and pants concealing 50 pounds of gear, their gym bags stuffed with ropes and two-way radios. In the elevator, they chatted idly. At the 13th floor they stepped out and silently climbed four stories to the roof. There, they...began rappelling down the office tower. Maneuvering through the air like trapeze artists, Parker and Gerhardt unfurled a gigantic banner: 'Stop the Rape of Mother Earth. Boycott Mitsubishi.'...When they finally climbed back to the roof, Mitsubishi had agreed to a meeting." ("Eco-warriors: Women Who Risk Their Lives for Your Future," *Marie Claire*, November 1997, pp. 44–46)

And to think I've wasted precious moments thinking about unwise sex, while those young women are out there putting their lives on the line for my sake. It makes me cringe. I vow to thank every hero I can find and ask how I can help with their work, since I'll be having more free time during my breakfast and lunch hours from now on.

Chapter Seven

The Art of Relaxing in the World

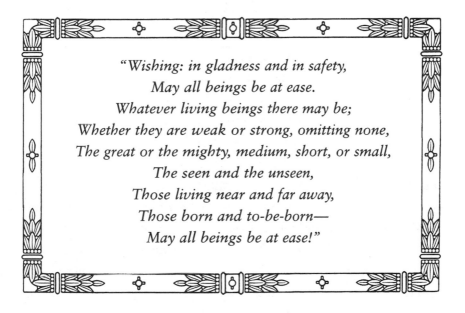

"Wishing: in gladness and in safety,
May all beings be at ease.
Whatever living beings there may be;
Whether they are weak or strong, omitting none,
The great or the mighty, medium, short, or small,
The seen and the unseen,
Those living near and far away,
Those born and to-be-born—
May all beings be at ease!"

Hours after hours continue to pass; swiftly the day and night are gone. Days after days continue to pass; swiftly the end of the month is gone. Months and months continue to pass; suddenly next year has arrived. Years after years continue to pass; unexpectedly we have arrived at the portal of death.

A broken cart cannot move. An old person cannot cultivate. Yet still we humans lie, lazy and indolent; still we humans sit, with minds distracted. How many lives have we not cultivated? Yet still we pass the day and night in vain. How many lives have we spent in our useless bodies? Yet still we do not cultivate in this lifetime either. This life must come to an end; but what of the next? Is this not urgent? Is this not urgent?

—The monk Wonhyo

(*Sourcebook of Korean Civilization, Volume 1: From Early Times to the Sixteenth Century,* edited by Peter H. Lee, New York: Columbia University Press, 1993)

We are so quick to judge each other: He's wise; she's a fool; he's stupid; she's my soul mate; she should be more like me; he should; they should. What if I told you that our judging serves no purpose except to cram our minds with idle chitchat? It's true: no useful purpose. Buddhism is chock-full of this teaching.

The story of Wonhyo is one example. Wonhyo lived in Korea in the seventh century (617–686). He wrote about 180 books before he died, on 87 different subjects covering most of the important schools of Buddhist thought. Raised in a prominent aristocratic family, Wonhyo quickly gained a reputation as a scholar. His first love was Confucianism, which he studied incessantly as a young boy. He then fell in love with Buddhism from the moment he was introduced to it, throwing himself into long periods of meditation, only taking breaks to study the sutras and rules of monastic living so he could make certain he was doing everything correctly. After years of intensive training, some of it in monasteries, Wonhyo had managed to make quite a name for himself as a Buddhist scholar. However, enlightenment was not his.

Frustrated, Wonhyo decided to go to China to find a Zen master who could coach him through the breakthrough that he couldn't seem to make on his own. He set off on foot, hiking over the Korean mountains, starting out each day before dawn and stopping only after the sunlight was completely gone. One night the young monk was so tired that he fell asleep before he even had time to start a fire to cook some food. During the night, terrorized by nightmares, he forced himself to wake up. Waking, he realized that he was wildly thirsty. As he rolled over, trying to see where he had fallen asleep, he noticed what looked like a silver goblet filled with water. Lifting it to his mouth he drank it dry, relishing its sweetness.

When he woke up the next morning, Wonhyo looked for the goblet, only to discover that "it was in fact a human skull filled with putrid, worm infested water. He realized in that instant that it was only his mind that made 'pure' and 'impure,' 'good' and 'evil.' With this insight he no longer felt there was a need to travel to China." (Peter D. Hershock, *Liberating Intimacy: Enlightenment and Social Virtuosity in Ch'an Buddhism*, Albany, N.Y.: State University of New York Press, 1996, p. 186)

Taken aback by that story, I was fascinated with Wonhyo and decided to learn more about him, including whether he lived through his next week. He did. In fact, he lived to a ripe old age, and was perhaps the most seminal Buddhist thinker in Korea. What I found was my new hero of heroes. A Zen wild man—Robin Williams in monk robes— and one of the most helpful teachers I've had the good fortune to stumble onto.

While other monks stayed in secluded monasteries, Wonhyo hit the streets. He played musical instruments in shrines and made up songs about Buddhism that lay people could understand, singing them at the top of his lungs in the villages he passed through. He taught everyone within hearing distance about Buddhism in what can only be described as a sixth-century version of pop-rock. To make a point he did tricks such as juggling food trays and spitting water out of his mouth to quench a fire. And unlike other monks, he would accept invitations from "commoners" to stay with them, instead of spending his nights in local monasteries.

One time he sang the same line for days: "Who'll lend me an ax without a handle? I'd like to chisel away at the pillar that supports heaven." As the reputation of this wildly eccentric and worldly-wise teacher spread, the local king, King Moyal, started to pay more attention to what he heard. The king decided that Wonhyo's mind should be a national treasure and sent some of his attendants to find the monk to bring him back to the palace. On the way back to the palace, Wonhyo deliberately fell into a river, soaking his clothes so he could slow down the speed of the trip. Since he only owned one set of clothing, the group was forced to spend the night at a nearby castle. In those days, any change of clothing was so rare that people would have to strip down and stay stripped until their clothes were dry. Without going into the romance-novel details, let me just say that Wonhyo managed to spend the night with the castle's resident princess. They conceived a son, Sol Ch'ong, who was both clever and intelligent.

Back to the story's hero. Wonhyo was not interested in being a national treasure and finally convinced the king that they would both be better off if Wonhyo was left alone to be who he was—a wandering monk. For twenty years he wandered throughout Korea, singing his songs and offering up entertaining teachings to the townspeople. Sol Ch'ong later became a counselor to the king in place of his father.

Over time, Wonhyo became increasingly frustrated at the depth of his own spiritual practice. Although he had experienced some spiritual insights, deep enlightenment continued to be elusive. Hearing about an old Zen master in the mountains, he decided to find him and ask for guidance. When Wonhyo reached the old man's retreat he found him weeping uncontrollably. He had found a baby deer whose mother had died giving birth. When the old monk had gone to the village to beg for milk for the doe, he had made up a story about getting a woman pregnant who had died giving birth to his son so people would give him milk. Instead of milk, all he got was rice and a scandalous reputation. Worse, when he returned to his hermitage he discovered that the fawn had died.

But Wonhyo knew he had found his teacher. The old master told Wonhyo that he would have to sacrifice everything he had if he was to have a true experience of enlightenment. When Wonhyo made the vow, the old man asked the young monk to join him for a walk and proceeded to take him straight to a brothel. There the house prostitute greeted them with a smile and prepared food and drink for a night of partying.

Wonhyo was stunned. This was crazier than anything he had ever done. Laughing at his reaction, the old monk told him that it isn't good to dwell in heaven for too long. Sometimes it is good to visit hell. Wonhyo argued back that spending time with the prostitute would be breaking precept after precept! Grinning, the old master looked at the prostitute and warned her that she would go straight to hell if she took Wonhyo in. Was she afraid?

Taking Wonhyo's hand, the woman replied that she knew Wonhyo would come down to save her if she did end up in hell. She trusted completely in the compassion of the monk standing before her.

As the story goes, they had quite a night together. The next morning, Wonhyo had a deep experience of enlightenment and was so thrilled that he rushed through the city streets shouting and singing. He had discovered one of the primary truths of our existence: When we are able to utterly give up our judgments, we will stumble into our own enlightenment. Although Wonhyo's teacher was rather unusually and unconventionally creative in pushing Wonhyo over the final cliff away from his judging mind, the man deserves credit. His strategy worked. With all judgment erased Wonhyo had at last found his own Buddha nature.

Wonhyo's teachings are so respected in the Korean Buddhist community that he is considered to be the teacher most responsible for developing a distinctively Korean approach to spiritual practice—an approach that is direct, accessible, and often wildly entertaining.

Let's be like Wonhyo. Let's be without judgment and watch how situations play out differently when we are free from ourselves, when we are truly at ease with the situation. Let's stop our needing to know, to categorize, to be sure.

Several summers ago, I gave myself the gift of attending a Hindu spiritual retreat for women. I found myself surrounded by women who simply weren't judging anything, they were just being. Over and over I was struck by the power of letting go of my mental models of how the world and everything in it ought to be. It became so clear to me how destructive our labels are—all of them.

There was an older woman staffing the retreat who really brought this home to me. My experience of her was that she was funny and smart with a deeply intuitive way of knowing when someone needed a hug, a blanket, or to be left alone. She normally spent her days working at an AIDS hospice program.

At lunch one day she told me her life story. It was overflowing with heartbreaks, with homelessness, with drugs. Most painful of all, she told me that she had spent most of her adult life in an insane asylum and had been written off by everyone until she met a spiritual teacher who had seen through the surface of her life to her innate compassion and her deep spirituality. The teacher helped her to get out of the asylum and return to the world as a deeply compassionate caregiver.

If we are going to be serious about this spiritual work, we must move out of our little ego-driven minds to our Mahayana, or great unknowing mind. Since I for one have no interest in drinking anything out of a skull in the hope of a deep spiritual awakening, my vote is that we learn from Wonhyo's experience and make the commitment to let go of what we think we know, so we can be open to the real truth of our experiences.

Buddha talked quite a bit about this letting go, but he warned that the shift is a gradual process. In one story, Buddha tells of a goldsmith learning to refine gold. To his great surprise, he discovers that the refining process has layers. The first one consists of getting rid of the rocks and the big stuff. In layer two, you deal with pebbles. The third layer consists of getting rid of grit that isn't gold. And in the fourth, dust that isn't gold dust. Only then is high-quality gold left.

Our penchant for judging everything can be similarly broken down. Happily, most of us have gotten rid of our "gross impurities" and discriminations. You know the ones: that we're smarter than everyone else we know; that people who are racists are totally evil; that our way is the best and right way. (In case you are frowning at the page, not quite sure if you really have ceased to make these gross judgments, even the early stages of meditation can be sufficient to accomplish this. So just spend more time meditating. They'll come to the surface and you can let them go.)

The second "pebbles" layer is more subtle. For example, we may secretly hope someone has a miserable day because he or she was nasty to us yesterday, or we hesitate to send our teenagers to a religion-based camp because they might be exposed to something we disagree with, not quite trusting that teenagers already know themselves and what to believe pretty well. Meditation will enable you to witness your judgmental thoughts. Eventually they will go away because they no longer have an impact on how you react to a given situation.

Learning more about whatever it is you are judging can be helpful, too. Nathan McCall, author of *Makes Me Wanna Holler,* has talked about how living in a house with white people taught him that every white person is not a racist. One of my hiking buddies, a self-labeled "red neck," never ceases to catch me in the middle of my own judging mind. I have watched his militarism over the years and, watching more closely, have seen how it reflects a deep, deep love for this country and a sincere concern for our children's future. It doesn't mean that we are on the same side of most political issues, but I appreciate him in a way I never would have without my practice.

Layer three is tougher. Buddha named this our layer of "fine impurities." Examples include a slight smugness about ourselves when we are admired, or thoughts related to not wanting to be disliked. Constantly watching each moment scrubs these thoughts clean. Such mindfulness takes training similar to the martial arts. We need to stick with it and, when we lose our focus, to just keep starting over until the mindfulness takes hold and we notice that the fine impurities are gone.

The fourth layer seems to take care of itself over time. When the mind settles into relaxed and constant mindfulness as a result of long-term meditation practice, even the dust that isn't gold lets go of its hold on us. Judgment is gone and in its place is openness. This is when our hearts grow big, becoming the driving force of our lives.

Knowing that we have these layers to work through, what can we do? Our job is to keep practicing our spirituality. Just like Wonhyo. And if we get stuck, there are hundreds of tools available to us and worlds of

Buddhas and bodhisattvas and saints ready to help. Sometimes I just stop and offer up any difficulties to Buddha, trusting that my letting go will help clean out my judging mind. Offer up the difficulties to whatever saint helps you. I'm happy to share Tara. Whatever god. Whatever Buddha. Sometimes I just ask this question out loud: "So what do I have to do to clear out this layer?" And wait for an answer to pop up in my head. Or I may ask a teacher. And then do what I know I have to do to get unstuck.

There are innumerable methods for brain clearing and inspiration all around us. Michael Kielb, a writer for the *Ann Arbor News*, recounts a classic week from hell. His new computer arrived and, within four hours of setting it up, there was a total systems failure and the computer company couldn't locate a replacement. Then, in a letter, the state of Michigan informed him that, after thirty-five years, it failed to recognize the social security number assigned to him by the federal government. Just as he was taking all these crises in, his ancient, kidney-diseased cat peed right on his foot. At that moment he heard a bird singing outside. "Sitting down, I closed my eyes and let this avian dwarf steal away my stress. This tiny songster had the power to remind me that there was more to life than the constraints and difficulties imposed by society. A single bird, soloist extraordinaire, took me from where I thought I was to where I wanted to be. I listened to the wren as I thought about the nonmonetary value of nature and the important role that birds and other animals and plants play in helping us to deal with the stresses of our everyday lives." (Michael Kielb, *Ann Arbor News*, November 1, 1997)

If I'm still stuck in dual thinking, in judgment, I revert back to a tried-and-true, if slightly bizarre, tactic. I call it my "Wonhyo solution." It works every time. I simply pretend that my teacher Sunim can read my mind. Just that thought makes me sit up straight and fly right. Just thinking of the possibility immediately erases judgment. And it doesn't hurt to have him look me in the eye every once in a while and say the very words I've been thinking. As soon as it happens, I plug in this vow: "May all beings be at ease. Whatever living beings they may be." He smiles. I smile back.

Chapter Eight

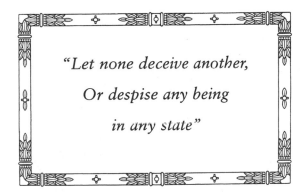

Why Lying Sucks

> "Let none deceive another,
> Or despise any being
> in any state"

A four-year-old was at the doctor's for a checkup. As the doctor looked in her ears he asked, "Do you think I'll find Big Bird in here?" The little girl stayed silent.

Next the doctor took a tongue depressor and looked down her throat. He asked, "Do you think I'll find the Cookie Monster down there?"

Again, silence.

Then the doctor put a stethoscope to her chest. As he listened to her heart beat, he asked, "Do you think I'll hear Barney in here?" "Oh no!" the little girl replied. "Jesus is in my heart. Barney's on my underpants."

(From an Internet email)

Let's be just like her. Buddha in our hearts and Barney on our underpants. Wide open. So honest that it doesn't even occur to us to lie. So honest that when someone listens to our hearts and asks what we'll find in there, we tell them the answer: love if it's love, hurt if it's hurt, panic if it's panic, and Barney if it's him.

When Buddha discovered his own enlightened heart, he had a lot of time to think about how to help the rest of us uncover the same truth. He could have left behind a thousand rules; instead his teachings were simple, short, and direct: *Live the eightfold path.* That's it and that's all. Be moral. Concentrate. Discover your wisdom so you can benefit all sentient beings. There are many renditions of this eightfold path, and it is worth the time it takes to hunt down several in search of your favorite. In the meantime, here's one version:

> Eightfold Path: The path leading to release from suffering. The eight parts of the path are: 1) right view, based on the under-standing of the Four Noble Truths and the non individuality of existence; 2) right resolve, in favor of renunciation, good will, and non harming of sentient beings; 3) right speech, or avoidance of lying, slander, and gossip; 4) right action, or avoidance of harm-ing sentient beings; 5) right livelihood, or avoidance of profes-sions that are harmful to sentient beings, such as butcher, hunter, weapons or narcotics dealer; 6) right effort, or cultivation of what is karmically wholesome and avoidance of what is karmically unwholesome; 7) right mindfulness, or ongoing mindfulness of body, feelings, thinking, and objects of thought; and 8) right con-centration, which finds its high point in meditative absorption.

> (*Entering the Stream: An Introduction to the Buddha and His Teachings,* edited by Samuel Bercholz and Sherab Chodzin Kohn, Boston: Shambhala Publications, 1993, p. 317)

Live the path. Embrace the intention of living your entire life from your heart for the benefit of not just yourself but everyone else sharing your lifetime. Think kind thoughts. Be honest. Be kind. Let your actions reflect your highest wisdom and let your livelihood be harmless. Con-centrate on your spiritual practice. Be mindful and share the wisdom that grows out of all the rest of it.

These guidelines are pretty user-friendly, so it's hard to pretend we don't understand them. But, vowing to follow them, beware: You'll slip and learn more about yourself than you probably want to. Where we trip up the worst is where we need to do our core work.

The surprise to me was that my speech is what gets me into the most trouble. Cursing aside, I find myself wanting to make up stuff in all sorts of situations far too often. Someone asks me out, and I go. Invariably the conversation shifts to our ages. I want to say I'm thirty-four. I can feel myself about to mouth the words .....th...ir...t...y...f.....ou......r....., but finally, after all these years of practice, I stop myself. I know that just that one lie will create a continuous obligation to build more lies, not to mention that I will set a precedent that lying is okay.

Or a client calls about a report that's due the next day that I haven't started. She wants reassurance that I'll meet the deadline and I want to lie to her, saying I'm proofing the draft. "What harm will it cause?" I ask myself. Well, the truth is, it could still be late and then the client would find out I wasn't telling the truth. I swallow hard and tell her that it is my top priority of the day and that I've just consumed three cups of green tea with ginseng for extra energy and I've never missed a deadline in my life. (I swear to myself that I'll start sooner with the next project.) She probably worries through the night, but I manage to get the report done. Appreciating my honesty, she gives me more work and I reflect on how difficult right speech can be.

One of the toughest situations that I deal with these days is that since my ordination people see me differently. Friends and acquaintances expect an ordained Zen teacher to know a lot more than I ever will. Short-term memory loss notwithstanding, I'm expected to know historical facts about the great Zen masters, how getting a cold connects back to spiritual practice, and all the words to all the chants.

Every Sunday I face this expectation head-on during our public service. There is a period when anyone at the service can ask the teacher any question related to Buddhism and his or her practice. It is a twenty-first century version of "dharma combat," where monks would argue about teachings in an effort to deepen their own spirituality. Most Sundays the questions are fun and remind me of the value of continued learning. But every once in a while I get one question after another that stumps me. I want to lie. I want to make up answers. Instead, frequently as an act of sheer will power, "I don't know" comes out of my mouth. Because I don't. Because the teaching is so clear: Let none deceive another. Cringing through a cascade of "I don't knows" one Sunday, I suddenly realized that my own stumbling gives everyone in our sangha an opportunity to really care about me just the way I am, without inflated ideas of what I know, since I'll never know enough.

Deception is utterly destructive and the damage can grow exponentially. Think of a time when you've lied. Looking back, didn't the ripples of repercussions far outweigh the price you might have paid had you told the truth in the first place? (Maybe it was just to yourself. Maybe it was that you needed to say to yourself, "He is going to physically hurt me" or "She is going to drink again.") I know that's always been true for me. Even in situations where I've paid a harsh personal price.

As I think about this, all of the great spiritual teachers that I can think of told us to be honest: Christ, Moses, Muhammad. Honesty, they say, offers a direct line to spiritual salvation and to peace. Be honest so your heart can stay open, they tell us.

In a recent survey of 40,000 adults in the United States, 93% admitted to lying regularly and habitually, in spite of personal costs that showed up in the form of stress, anxiety, deteriorating relationships, and worse. (Alice Van Housen, "Here's a Radical Idea—Tell the Truth," *Fast Company,* August/September 1997, p. 50) The biggest price we pay is that when we lie, we stop trusting everyone else as well. It's not only that our spiritual practice could only be more damaged if we drove over it with a truck, it's that it has an impact on everything in our lives.

Not long ago, Dr. Steven Berglas, a psychologist on the faculty of the Harvard Medical School, worked on a project where he had to help a business genius to stop sexually harassing his female staff.

"Look," the genius said to me during our first meeting, "I don't need your help. I'm going to trial on these sexual-harassment

charges, and I'm going to lie. What's more, my two top execu-
tives have agreed to lie for me. Hell, I could tell all my workers
that I'm intending to lie under oath and it wouldn't make a damn
bit of difference. Cash, stock in the company, they're what matter today. What makes you think integrity matters? President
Clinton dances around the truth daily. If integrity mattered, Dole
would be President."

The genius reasoned that if the President could get away with his
alleged bad behavior, then why couldn't he? But the genius missed
the point. A chief executive may adhere to the mandate "Do as I
say, not as I do," but most people behave according to the prin-
ciple that actions speak louder than words....When you lie and
believe there will be no consequences for your leadership status or
your bottom line, if your key workers are spineless and mercenary
too, then you may be correct. Lawyers will tell you that the courts
are so full of pathological prevaricators that judges and arbitrators
have come to believe that everyone who stands before them is at
least mildly disingenuous. The CEO who lies and cheats, however,
should remember this: The liar's punishment is not that he is not
believed, but that he can believe no one else.

(Steven Berglas, "Liar, Liar, Pants on Fire," *Inc.*, August 1997)

Brad Blanton is another psychologist who has studied the consequences of lying. His focus has been on business as well. Over time Brad
has become a one-man Joan of Arc preaching radical honesty to anyone
who will listen: "'We lie all the time and it wears us out....We manage
our companies through a series of delusional cliches: "The customer is
always right"; "I'm not angry"; "We're proceeding according to plan."
But we all know better than that. Lying takes a huge toll in terms of stress,
anxiety, and depression.'" ("Here's a Radical Idea—Tell the Truth")

This is a good day to make a vow to shift to a life of radical honesty.
To tell the truth...not to deceive...ever. When we make such a promise
to ourselves, our lives lighten up dramatically and things get better all
around us. Mary Cusack was given the job of starting up a $50 million

packaging plant for Procter & Gamble's Light Duty Liquids such as Dawn, Joy, and Ivory. When she started planning, she quickly realized that her working environment was a cauldron of dishonesty and distrust. She decided that the only way to get the project done successfully was to refuse to be anything but honest herself, and to encourage her whole team to do the same. And it worked. They completed the project successfully, in record time, for $10 million less than projected. Her brilliant method? She got people to look each other in the eye, share their resentments and appreciation, and move on. ("Here's a Radical Idea—Tell the Truth")

Fortunately, most of us don't have to buck entire corporate cultures, only our own habits and our own fears. The way to be honest is simply to *be honest*. Let's promise ourselves and each other that we will really try to tell the truth about everything in our lives, all the time.

Let none of us deceive another.

Honesty makes things better because it offers the opportunity to live a life of deep integrity. Honesty lets me deal directly with the reality of my life rather than what I choose to believe is going on. Such reality checks have always changed my life for the better, sometimes sooner, sometimes later. Radical honesty is the best because then there's no guessing about a given situation. This saves an inordinate amount of anguish, not to mention clothes shopping, binge eating, and the renting of a dozen romantic movies at a time.

Honesty makes things better. In the *Therigatha*, a collection of ancient poems about the first women followers of Buddha, there is a heart-wrenching love story of a young woman, Capa, and a young monk, Kala. Apparently, he used to show up at her house on his daily begging rounds. Kala never saw Capa because her father always met him at the door with a generous offering of food. But, deciding that Capa was old enough to manage the household, her father went off hunting for a week. Seeing Capa at the door the next morning, Kala fell head over heels in love (I have a feeling William Shakespeare got many of his best ideas from the *Therigatha*) and vowed to starve himself to death if he could not make her his bride.

Since he had also made a vow of silence, Kala didn't bother to mention this to anyone, and instead went into the forest to starve himself to death. Fortunately, Capa's father returned from his hunting trip and asked about the young monk, only to be told that he hadn't been seen for several days. Concerned, he went to find Kala, who told him of his feelings for Capa. So struck was he by the young man's fervor that Capa was given to him in marriage. Since he was exceedingly good looking (just a guess), Capa proceeded to fall head over heels back. They married and had a son.

So far, so good. Unfortunately, over time Kala realized that his true yearning really was to live an utterly spiritual life. In an effort to protect Capa from his thoughts, he didn't say anything. Instead, their marriage deteriorated to the point at which they were both miserable. And Capa blamed herself for their problems, having no idea what she could do better. (Does this sound familiar?)

Finally, Kala told his wife the truth, that he had to renounce the world, to live again as a monk.

Heartbreak.

But once she knew what she was dealing with, Capa was able to free herself of self-blame. Their problems weren't about her. It helped, of course, that Kala told her that she was not only beautiful but also a good mother to their son. Offered the truth of the situation, she was able to really observe her husband and start to understand the deep tugging at his heart. Freeing him from what was an untenable commitment, Capa then started listening more carefully to the teachings of Buddha. She began to undertake her own spiritual practice, and she became one of the first women to discover her own enlightened heart—giving the rest of us hope, not to mention one heck of a role model. Years later, Capa died in a state of transcendent joy, deeply grateful for Kala's honesty.

Radical honesty is not about going off at the mouth in every situation. The wisdom that grows out of your spiritual practice will tell you when your own attachments are skewing your clarity. Maybe you are hurt, or angry, or sad, or just plain want an emotional win. In those moments, silence works. Silence gives us a much needed distancing so we can more clearly see the truth of a given situation. I have learned, for example, that it is much better for me just to keep my mouth shut on *any topic related to any relationship I'm in* (daughter, parent, best friend, teacher, student, mate, business) from two days before a full moon until two days afterward. My reactions to situations are just too exaggerated otherwise. My hormones are too strong. When I don't keep my mouth shut, I invariably find myself cleaning up after my righteous need for honesty. Until I started watching myself, I never noticed the chaos I was creating in that five- to six-day window. Now I know. Now I'm quiet. If there is a truth to be talked about or acted upon, it will still be there in a few days.

Here's the thing. You have a similar window to watch out for. Maybe it's around the moon cycles, maybe it is before and after you pay monthly bills, or maybe it revolves around work-related activities. Being honest in these situations means waiting out the emotional storm so you can really see what is going on.

Let none deceive another. Here's another example of the deep healing made possible with radical honesty. There is a piece of paradise in Florida: Its name is Kashi Ashram. Alive with songbirds and frogs and quiet laughter. The people who live at Kashi are saints, although they don't look like saints exactly. Some look like gently aging hippies with their long hair and flowing clothing; some are children; some look like they could play lead roles in just about any adventure series on television; and a few are ancient.

What you notice about them all is their eyes. They shine. And they smile. Mostly, though, they heal. If you go there for a retreat, these saint-beings help you to heal. If you are dying from AIDS, they house you. The healing is subtle: a touch, a grin, or just walking close to you when you are on the verge of understanding a depression that you have carried for decades. It is an amazing place.

Their teacher—their guru—is a woman who first stumbled onto her own spiritual self as a heavy (as in almost three hundred pounds) Jewish housewife who went to a Yoga class to learn a breathing technique that her friends had been using to lose weight. When she tried this breathing she had visions and even visitations from Jesus Christ and various saints from other religions. It almost made her crazy. But out the other end emerged one heck of a teacher. She doesn't look exactly like what most of us think an enlightened being should look like, with her heavy makeup, loads of jewelry, and flat-out flashiness, but an extraordinary teacher, nonetheless.

This woman does not beat around any bushes. She will single out someone in a crowd and directly address a problem that person has faced for years. Then she calls it the way she sees it. Her students call it "the killing"—she goes for the jugular of the problem and cuts right into it, surrounding her surgery with a deep and abiding compassion. People let go of deep emotional pain, of the lies they have lived with, of fear. I am in awe.

Let's promise each other to live our lives with as much honesty as we can muster. Promise me you will try to tell the truth about everything and I promise the same right back. Just keep starting over whenever you find yourself ducking an opportunity to be honest. And yes, I still cringe when a good friend asks me how she looks in a new suit, hairstyle, relationship, and my reaction is that she could do a lot better. Some part of me continues to feel morally obligated to exaggerate a point if it will help me to win an argument. But I remind myself of this sutra. And am glad of it.

Let none deceive another. Tell the truth compulsively, says Brad Blanton. Tell the truth about everything, if you can: what you are planning, where you've been, whether your stomach hurts, if you are upset. The trick is to be descriptive and precise.

Here's an example of what I mean. A friend of mine worked incredibly hard on a marketing campaign and came up with some breakthrough ideas for his firm. At the meeting where he was supposed to present his ideas to top management, his manager stood up and proceeded to make the whole presentation of the proposed campaign himself, implying that he had done all the preparations himself. After the meeting, my friend went for a long walk, checked the phases of the moon, decided that his reactions to the situation were true, and went in to talk to his manager.

Here is a paraphrasing of what he said: "I am very angry that you implied that you solely created our marketing campaign after the months of work I've put into it. It makes me feel like I can't trust you and that we can't work together. Right now I feel like I am going to have to keep my creative ideas to myself. I don't think this is good for the team or the firm."

His boss, surprised, apologized and immediately sent out an all-points email extolling my friend and the hard work he had been doing. What is interesting about this story is that my friend was able to let the situation go and his boss started to pay closer attention to his own behavior, since he didn't want to lose one of his best staff. Months later, when I asked how things were, my friend replied: "You know, I honestly think he didn't realize how he sounded at that meeting, he was so determined to get a go-ahead for the campaign." Without that conversation you know what would have happened. My friend probably would have left the company, and everyone involved would have been hurt. So let's tell the truth, *please*, and if we have to repeat it to be heard, let's repeat it. There's time.

In a life lived honestly, respect for all beings grows and the straightforwardness we all want for our lives surfaces. Other people's trust in us grows as they realize that if we aren't saying something is bothering us, then we really aren't bothered. So they don't need to dodge, avoid, or tiptoe around us. Best of all, we don't ever have to remember what we said to cover for ourselves, because we know that whatever we said or did was our truth at that moment. Blanton takes the benefits a step further: "'Once people get through to the truth, they fall in love with it.'" ("Here's a Radical Idea—Tell the Truth")

You decide. Speaking the truth is like Drano working on the clogs and snags of our hearts. It eats away at the crud that is blocking our innate loving-kindness. Without loving-kindness there is no joy. Who wants that life?

Chapter Nine

How Buddhists Can Help Save the Spirit of Christmas

"Let none through anger

or ill will

Wish harm upon another"

I can just picture Mary, the mother of Jesus, happy ever after in her heaven, looking down at the mess we humans have made of things on earth, turning to Jesus and saying, "That place is a wreck! Get down there and remind those people what real love is all about." And did he ever. It is an extraordinary story, the life of Christ, because it reminds each of us of our deep capacity to cherish each other and to take care of what we've been given. Celebrate his birth every year? I'm in.

The spirit of Christmas matters. That's why I love Christmas. I love it because—for many of us, Christians and non-Christians alike—it is a season that applauds our acting from our hearts. Maybe it's just for one day, but somewhere in there, our whole deluded society puts itself on pause to be kind in some way. And it's the only time we do, really, in such large numbers, anyway.

As a little girl I remember magical moments during the holiday season. I remember waking up with my sisters long before daylight on a December Saturday to sneak around and shovel all the sidewalks in sight. I remember the special phone calls and cards. Every Christmas season, my friend Deb Elmore, who is nonreligious to her bones, heads to the nearest toy store, buys enough toys to fill her truck, and then delivers them to local churches where children may not be having much of a Christmas. Last year she pulled up at a church she had never visited before, just after the minister had discovered that all of the toys and gifts his congregation had gathered had been stolen. It was Christmas Eve.

Without the annual Christmas season where would we be? Aside from the retailers who would go bankrupt, it could be too easy to forget about the value of generosity and how much you and I are nourished by it—as givers and receivers. The busyness that has flattened patience, appreciation, and kindness needs the antidote we call Christmas, now more than ever.

So where do we Buddhist types fit in? How can we help keep the spirit of Christmas strong and maybe even stretch it right past the holiday season? In two ways. Buddha taught that by living our lives in four "heavenly abodes" we could protect and nourish our naturally generous spirits. So the first thing you and I can do is focus more attention on these abodes, ever watchful for opportunities to practice them. What are they? The first is equanimity: calmness. Recalling the hysteria of most of my Christmases past, a little equanimity goes a long way. This is not a passive calmness, but a warrior calmness. Like being okay with sitting in the eye of a hurricane and then being okay when the eye suddenly shifts to the hurricane itself. No matter what, calmness.

There is a story of an old monk who woke up one morning to find a young pregnant girl at his doorstep. She told him she needed a place to live. "Is that so?" he said and took her in. She then ran away and had the baby, and when her parents demanded to know who the father was, she told them it was the old monk. Furious, they rushed to his cottage accusing him of immoral, reprehensible behavior. "Is that so?" he replied. They demanded he care for the girl and her baby. So he did.

Years later, the girl, feeling remorse, confessed to her parents that another man was the child's father. Mortified, her parents went to the monk to beg for forgiveness. Deeply apologetic, they told him of the girl's confession. "Is that so?" he responded. And continued to care for the girl and her child until his death.

Let's be like him.

The second abode is joy. The Christmas season offers all manner of excuses for joy: that we are alive; that yesterday was yesterday but not today; that we have a place to sleep; that the stars come out and the sun still rises, and we usually have heat when we want it; that the phone mostly works, and the car mostly runs, and we can still taste our food. Joy in the stories of Christmas that we all hear and in the fun and funny sayings that surface in this season. "You better not pout, you better not cry." For all the Kodak moments and the wide-open excuse to be as childlike as we can let ourselves be.

Then there is the abode of compassion. This is the third abode we can bring into this season, we followers of the Buddha's footsteps. In our practice of compassion we can sense when someone needs a foot rub, or a nap, or a break from a too long "to do" list. We can empathize with the inevitable hurts that surface with the season, like the mother who still can't accept that her daughter is a lesbian or a brother who still won't forgive his best friend for marrying his sister.

The fourth abode? Back to loving-kindness. Heart-driven friendliness. Here's where we need to remember that everyone (yes, everyone) is our friend. Some of the people in our lives are our friends because they stand by us in our most difficult moments, and some of the people are our friends because they create our most difficult moments. Either way, our own open friendliness makes the world turn a bit more gently and feeds the fire of Christmas so it can last.

The Buddhist concept of friendliness represents the enduring friendship that is present in both grief and joy, and that is at its very core a manifestation of that unconditional love that you and I want. In this abode it is impossible for us to wish harm on each other because ill will is absent. We are friends and that is that. And even if we get angry, we don't wish harm. We wish for an end to the anger.

The Buddha taught that this friendship is a summary statement of the good life because it draws into it the other abodes—equanimity, joy, and compassion. In an often told story, Buddha's attendant Ananda approaches him, pleased at a sudden insight. He says, "Buddha, friendship is half of all that matters, isn't it?" To which Buddha replies, "No, Ananda, friendship is everything."

The Dalai Lama's whole life story is a demonstration of the power of friendliness. He is everyone's friend. When you meet him face to face, he grins at you like you are his long-lost best friend, looking deeply into your eyes with a kindness that is breathtaking. He laughs with everyone all the time, the way best friends do. John Cleese, formerly of *Monty Python* fame and now a business consultant, once talked about this with the Dalai Lama: "I asked him why it is that, in Tibetan Buddhism, they all laugh so much. It's the most delightful thing to be around them, because they are constantly in fits of giggles. And he said to me, very seriously, that laughter is very helpful to him in teaching and indeed in political negotiations, because when people laugh, it is easier for them to admit new ideas to their minds." (John Cleese, "Test: Can You Laugh at His Advice?" *Fortune Magazine*, July 6, 1998, p. 203)

Cleese is right about the giggling. The Parliament of World Religions meets every one hundred years. When it was held in Chicago several years ago, one of my jobs was to escort a handful of monks from Asia around downtown. The monks were quite elderly; the youngest looked to be in his mid-seventies. They smiled and giggled often. One of them, one of the oldest of the group, whenever he first saw me, would grin from ear to ear, point at me and shout "Smiling Girl," and break into a fit of giggling. His eyes just twinkled and he would circle me and bow and bow and bow and I would bow back until we were both dizzy and grinning at each other like schoolyard chums. They were all like that, those monks. For me, each day of the parliament was like spending time with my best friends in the whole world, even though we had never seen each other before, didn't really say more than a few words to each other, and haven't seen each other since. Not even a letter. But I know if I saw any of the group tomorrow, I would be "Smiling Girl" and we would go off, best buddies, into a shared adventure that I at least would remember forever. Such friendliness has the capacity to keep the Christmas fires burning throughout all time.

The four abodes. They nurture and protect us, protect the people we love, and protect the spirit of Christmas. They come highly recommended.

There is a second way we can play a role in this Yuletide pageant. We can make a vow to practice what our sangha calls "The Six Fingers of Zen," or the six paramitas. *Paramitas* are perfections. As such, they offer the basic ground rules for living each moment of our lives fully. They can keep us out of trouble and in the abodes, and are heartily recommended for an honored position on any Christmas season lover's refrigerator. Here is a list for yours:

Dana Paramita
May I be generous and helpful.

Sila Paramita
May I be pure and virtuous.

Ksanti Paramita
May I be patient. May I be able to bear and forbear
the wrongs of others.

Virya Paramita
May I be strenuous, energetic, and persevering.

Dhyana Paramita
May I practice meditation and attain concentration
and oneness to serve all beings.

Prajna Paramita
May I gain wisdom and be able to give the benefit
of my wisdom to others.

After so many years of reciting the paramitas, they feel rather self-explanatory. Even so, I propose that there are three actions that naturally flow out of these perfections and that can stretch out the Christmas season for months—maybe even as far as the next Christmas season, if we are really skillful.

First, let's be the best listeners ever. Let's be the ones who don't interrupt anyone who is talking to us, and let's be the ones who really care about the words being said. A pen pal of mine in Las Vegas, Kristopher, wrote me a letter in which he made an eloquent case for listening as the deepest act of compassion: "The most profound impression I get is that compassion is never so much of giving as it is of mindfulness, or attention. I don't know many who, at one time or another in their lives, haven't felt unappreciated…invisible. A simple act of someone just listening can change that, and that is what we are entitled to, and the least we can give. But then there is that matter of time and my schedule, huh? Then we are left with (a) the opportunity we just passed up and (b) the knowledge that it will never come again. Sort of a self-scoring, self-regulating testing mechanism."

I love Kristopher. He is wise. And he is right. We underestimate this simple gift and its capacity for creating miracles. Joan Halifax, a medical anthropologist and author who works with dying people, often talks about the gift of listening: "Most of what we are 'doing' is listening…. We're not giving advice. We're not doing psychotherapy. We're not administering medications. We are being present. And that presence requires listening—to what is said, what isn't said, even to silence. One person I worked with, a very wonderful man, had just gotten discharged from the hospital, and he said, 'Thirty, forty, fifty people come to see me in a typical hospital day, asking me questions. Not one person sat in silence with me, and that's all I wanted. Just somebody to be with me.' That's our true work." (Joan Halifax, *Tricycle*, Fall 1997, p. 62)

The second thing we can do? Surprise! Manual work. When I was little I would drive my mother nuts asking her to tell me the story of the littlest angel. Every Christmas Eve when I couldn't sleep, I would sneak into my parents' room, wake my mother up, and ask her if she could just tell me the story one more time. I usually repeated this ritual five or six times until dawn. Here's how I remember the story through a haze of forty years:

When Jesus was born, all the angels wanted to help out, so God gave them all important jobs. Some were guardian angels. Some came down to earth to guide Mary and Joseph. Some surrounded the stable where Jesus would be born to protect it. By the time the littlest angel got to the front of the line, there wasn't anything left to do.

Determined to be a part of this auspicious occasion, she begged God to let her go down to earth. He looked at his chore list to see if anything had been missed. Everything was covered. In tears the littlest angel started to turn away. Then, an idea. "You know, God, I'll bet the floor of that barn is pretty dirty. Could I go down and clean it and make sure the straw is nice and neat?" Permission granted. So down she came and she cleaned her heart out. When the divine baby was born, he smiled at all the angels in gratitude, but the biggest smile of all went to the littlest angel.

Aside from the fact that my mother was permanently programming me to clean her house on a regular basis, the lesson is a meaningful one. We can help each other in so many ways outside of buying gifts or going places. Let's clean for each other. Let's clean our parents' kitchens and bathrooms. Let's stack someone's wood or wash their car. And then let's move out from there. We can paint our little sister's room as a surprise and build a Beanie Baby house for the little girl we see standing at the bus stop each day. We can polish our brother's car or grease our father's lawn mower.

When did you and I lose touch with these deep acts of compassion? Not only is manual work meditative practice, it is also a reminder of how bountiful all of our lives are. Plus it offers an opportunity to help people we care about to sort and sift through their lives in a safe way, hopefully letting go of the things that no longer serve their lives in any meaningful way. My daughter and I "go manual" every Christmas season. We clean out closets, scrub around the edges of floors, repaint walls, and fill in nail holes throughout our apartment. Sometimes we get so carried away that we lose an entire weekend—and our apartment only has four rooms! Each year we rediscover books, and memories, and clothing we had forgotten existed. And we are refreshed, not exhausted, by the work. Clean, chop, cook, scrub. You'll love it once you get into it. Put on your favorite music, if you need a push, and just get started. The rest will take care of itself.

Several years ago, an acquaintance called me one November just to "check in." There was something in her voice that made me nervous. It was more than a deep sadness, there was this edgy, despairing undertone. Uncertain how to respond, I told her I was in a mood to do some cleaning and wondered if she had some chores that needed doing. Silence. She was probably checking to see if she had called the right number and whether to just hang up. Then a slight sigh. Then, "Yeah, come on over."

We scrubbed her floors. We didn't talk much—it was pretty weird. When we were done, I stayed for tea and drove home trying to figure out what was going on. Nothing surfaced, and eventually I got busy with the holiday season. A year later she checked in again. It was the same week. She told me that the purpose of her original call had been to say goodbye because she had decided to commit suicide. (I still don't know why.) But for some reason, scrubbing the floors triggered thoughts of the good things in her life—her cat, her job, her health. So she kept going, sought help, and moved to a smaller house, where she scrubs her floors whenever she feels like she is losing it. Manual work.

The third way we can keep the spirit of Christmas alive? Pure acts of generosity. The Buddha once said, "If you only knew the benefits of generosity, you would never eat a meal without sharing it." Little acts, middle-sized acts, big acts—they all count. In Illinois several years ago, a young girl with a rare blood type became ill with a life-threatening disease. She needed a blood transplant. The only possible donor found was her six-year-old brother. Asked if he would donate his blood to his sister, the little boy said he would like to think about it first. After a few days he agreed. In the hospital room next to his sister, he watched as the doctor drew blood from his arm and inserted a needle in his sister's arm. Within minutes color poured back into her cheeks. Seeing this, the boy asked the doctor, "Will I start to die right away?" (Jack Kornfield and Christina Feldman, *Soul Food: Stories to Nourish the Spirit and the Heart*, rev. ed., San Francisco: Harper San Francisco, 1996, p. 11)

Maybe we don't quite have that boy's courage in this lifetime. But we can visit hospitals. And we can pick up the ever expanding trash we see in the streets. We can be secret Santas and we can thank the people around us who are living with our karmic dispositions.

This season is for all of us. It's about getting back on our "heart track." As for me, every Christmas I thank the skies that someone in Rome, somewhere around 366 A.D. said, "I think we should celebrate Christmas to balance out those orgies." Amen.

Chapter Ten

माँ

Tap Dancing
in Zen

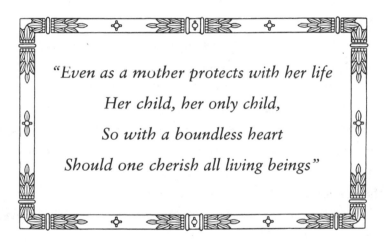

"Even as a mother protects with her life
Her child, her only child,
So with a boundless heart
Should one cherish all living beings"

As Buddha sat under the Bodhi tree at Bodh Gaya, determined to come to an understanding of why we all suffer and how we can end this suffering, amazing things happened to him. One was that he saw, with absolute clarity, all of his past lives. In his later teachings he would occasionally share tidbits from these lives to make a point. Many had to do with cherishing other sentient beings.

In one of the lifetimes, Buddha was born into a family of Brahmins known for their loving-kindness. Buddha himself was pretty lucky in that round. He was a smart, talented, healthy male who loved to spend time in the woods, sometimes in prayer, and sometimes simply enjoying being in the woods. One day he was walking with a friend up a steep mountain trail to a spot well suited to spiritual practice. As he passed a deep ravine he heard a roar. Looking down into the gulch, the young Brahmin saw the starved body of a young mother tiger. It was obvious that she hadn't eaten in a while and was suffering deeply. She was so hungry she was actually looking at her own offspring as food.

Shaken by the sight of such suffering, the young man turned to his friend and asked if he would help find some food for the mother and her cubs. When the friend ran off, the Brahmin stood there staring at the tigers. "I cannot feel pleasure while another being suffers, and if I have the power to help, how can I be indifferent? Even if the one who was suffering had committed the greatest crime, I could not withhold my aid; my heart would burn with remorse as readily as dry shrubs catch fire."

And then, to the amazement of even the gods, the young Brahmin threw himself over the edge of the cliff. When his friend returned empty-handed to the spot where they had seen the tigress and her cubs, he looked down only to see her devouring his friend. His reaction: "How merciful the Great Being was to beings in distress, and how indifferent to his own welfare! How heroic and fearless his immense love! He has perfected the conduct of the virtuous!" (Aryasura, *The Marvelous Companion: Life Stories of the Buddha*, Berkeley, Calif.: Dharma Publishing, 1983)

Like the young Brahmin, there are people throwing themselves off cliffs every day on behalf of the rest of us. Maybe they are flying a plane in a thunderstorm, trying to get a sick baby to a hospital. Maybe they are students publicly protesting an utterly corrupt government. Maybe it's mothers lying across a road every morning so a toxic-waste-filled truck won't dump the waste into their water supply. Maybe it's an entire city that decides to post "I'm a Jew" stickers on front doors to put a brake on an emerging neo-Nazi movement in their community.

Cherishing matters. It means holding something, or someone, dear. It is a love beyond bounds, beyond obsession. It is a risky love because it demands that we get out of our own self-focus and act on our innate knowing of what is right. It's downright scary.

But it's okay because we're up to it. We just need reminding. Here is one of my favorite stories that teaches us what love beyond bounds feels like. I wish I could remember where I first heard it, but I don't. Anyway, once upon a time, there were two old, really old, close to one hundred years old probably, friends named Asan and Hasan. They lived on the steppes of Russia. Asan had a little garden that managed to feed him and his daughter (his wife had died) and provide a few vegetables to sell for other necessities. For his part, Hasan had a horse that he could rent out for a small fee so he could buy vegetables for himself and his son (his wife was also dead). Well, as is true in most folktales, disaster struck. The horse died. Hasan was so heartbroken that he wanted to kill himself. But Asan, learning the news, said to his dear old friend, "Hasan, I will share my field with you. If we are very careful we will be able to feed all of us." So they were and they did.

One day Hasan's hoe hit something hard. He dug feverishly and in no time he had dug up a pot of gold. Mad with joy, he carried it to Asan to give it to him. But Asan said, "No, it isn't mine. You found it on your half of the land." Hasan argued that it had originally been Asan's land and he didn't want it.

Suddenly they looked at each other, the same thought crossing both their minds. The two men decided to offer it to their children on the condition that they marry each other. Off they went to Asan's daughter and Hasan's son to ask them if they would consider getting married so they could share the gold and never be poor again.

Since the daughter and son had been in love for years (not that their fathers had noticed), it was easy to say yes. But the next day they showed up at Asan's and then Hasan's to say they didn't want the gold either. For them love was enough.

And besides, the tiny plot of land was doing just fine feeding the four of them.

What to do with the gold? Asan and Hasan decided to take it to the king to let him decide how it could best be used. When they got to the king's palace, he just happened to be meeting with his four key advisers.

Asan and Hasan showed them the gold and asked for their advice. The king turned to his advisers. The first replied that the king should keep it in the castle, because you just never knew when some extra gold would come in handy. The king frowned.

The second adviser said that the king should use the gold to pay off his taxes, since the IRS had a reputation for being pretty hard on tax-evading kings. The king's frown deepened. The third adviser mentioned that it had been years since the advisers had received a raise. The king ignored him. Turning to the fourth and youngest adviser, he asked, "What do you say, young woman?"

She looked at him. Nervous because she was fresh out of adviser school, she said to the king, "Forgive my simplicity, but this is what I would do. With this gold I would buy seeds, and with the seeds I would plant in the barrenmost part of the steppe a vast and shaded garden, so that all the tired and weary poor might rest there and enjoy its fruits."

The king smiled at her compassion. "Just do it," he said, starting a very famous sports saying.

The best seeds could be purchased from a village many, many miles away. Since the youngest adviser was fearless, off she went, ready to face any danger. Happily the trip was without incident. But when she finally got to the village she heard horrible shrieking. And as she turned the corner into the village square, all she could see were camels laden with thousands and thousands of live birds—birds of the mountains and the forests, the steppes and the deserts. They were tied by their feet and, though they were trying to fly away, it was useless. They were bound so tightly they couldn't move. They could only shriek.

The young adviser was heartbroken. Approaching the caravan leader, she asked, "What would it take to free the birds?" He looked at her and laughed the deep belly laugh of a mean and awful caravan leader from one of the hell realms and spat out, "A pot of gold."

She smiled. "Fortunately, I just happen to have one with me." Stunned, he took her gold, freed the birds, and caravanned off into the sunset. The adviser was happy for the freed birds. Sighing with pleasure, she watched them fly away in the opposite direction from the caravan leader.

But what would she tell the king? What would she tell Asan and Hasan and their children? As she slowly, really, really slowly, walked back to the castle, her mood became gloomier and gloomier. Arriving at the castle, she took a deep breath and told the king what had happened. He didn't smile upon hearing the news. Instead, he told her, "Well, you'll need to go and tell Asan and Hasan what happened. They have already told all the villagers of the vision for a garden and a celebration is being planned."

The youngest adviser started out for Asan's and Hasan's in despair. Finally, night fell. Since she hadn't quite reached the old men's homes, she decided to sleep. Weeping, she wished she could figure out something, but her mind was a blank. As she closed her eyes, a beautiful bright-colored bird landed on her leg. And lo and behold, it started to sing in words the young woman could understand. "Forget your sorrow! We cannot return the gold to you. But we can reward your kindness in another way. Open your eyes and what you will see will dry your tears at once."

And when she did, what astonishment! The whole steppe was covered with birds scratching the earth with their claws, dropping seeds into the holes they were making with their beaks. And already seedlings were appearing. As the young woman watched, the most splendid garden imaginable rose before her very eyes. All she could do was laugh with joy. There were apples and grapes, shady paths, tulips and kale, and rose gardens. She leapt up and started to dance and the birds danced with her, singing and soaring in the sky.

Of course, all the commotion was so loud that it woke up Asan and Hasan and their children, not to mention everyone in the surrounding countryside. They all came running and, stunned at the beauty of the garden, began dancing and singing with the birds and the adviser. Even the king and all of his advisers (except for the one who wanted the raise) danced when they heard the news. And they all lived happily ever after.

If we live from our hearts, all things are possible. Gardens and songs and a life of extraordinary happiness. Miracles can happen. We can see our lives clearly. And we can love each other honestly. But when we live from our minds, none of these things are possible. Because our minds judge and protect and plan and worry *and need to be right*. We need to believe that what we *think* the world is like is really what it's like. So we miss the gardens, and the happy, unexpected endings, and the joy of the mystery.

If you can only give one gift to the world, let it be this: to live more from your heart and less from your mind. Let mystery in. Along with not-knowing. Let other people have an opportunity to be kind, and be on the alert for your own opportunities. In this shifting, you may just find the most amazing solutions to the most intractable problems in your life. Who knows? You might become so deliriously happy about your life that you'll look down to see your own feet tap dancing in Zen.

Chapter Eleven

Love
Beyond Boundaries

"*Radiating kindness over*
the entire world:
Spreading upwards to the skies,
And downwards to the depths;
Outward and unbounded"

According to the Mahayana Buddhist tradition, our Buddha nature is the true immutable and eternal nature of all of us. Because we all possess it, it is possible for each of us to attain enlightenment. The irony of this truth is that realization of our inherent Buddha nature does not grow out of grandiose acts, but from small, steady, selfless movements—an act of kindness here, a concentrated meditation sitting there, an hour of prayer, a thoughtful, healthy meal.

One of the most surprising stories from Buddha's own life was a visit he had from a king who wanted to check in with Sakyamuni to see how much merit he had earned so far in his lifetime. He had given away miles of land, food for whole villages, clothing for hundreds of families.

95

Buddha looked at him. "None." No merit. The king had been too self-serving. His gifts were too political, too self-aggrandizing. He had to start over with small acts of genuine kindness that would naturally grow and expand until the king himself radiated kindness. Then, and only then, would merit accumulate.

Some of Buddha's most powerful teachings were his own acts of kindness. When, as a young man, he was just emerging as a teacher, Buddha spent most of his time walking along the Ganges River, stopping in villages along the way to give dharma talks. In one community he spotted Sunita, a man responsible for carrying "night soil" from wealthy family homes to the outskirts of town for disposal. An untouchable, Sunita was covered in filth and stank like an outhouse on a sunny summer afternoon. When he saw Buddha, he immediately moved to get out of the way, veering toward the river so he could wash himself off.

Instead of ignoring Sunita, Buddha followed him. The other monks watched silently, unsure of their teacher's intentions. Curious villagers came out of their homes and lined the shore to watch what was happening. Sunita had veered off the path because he was afraid he would pollute the *bhikkhus* (monks). He could not have guessed Buddha would follow him. Sunita knew that the sangha included many men from noble castes. He was sure that polluting a bhikkhu was an unforgivable act. He hoped that Buddha and the bhikkhus would leave him and return to the road. But Buddha did not leave. He walked right up to the water's edge and said, "My friend, please come closer so we may talk." (Thich Nhat Hanh, *Old Path White Clouds: Walking in the Footsteps of the Buddha*, Berkeley, Calif.: Parallax Press, 1990)

Ignoring the rules of the caste system, Buddha invited Sunita to become a monk, a bhikkhu, right then and there. When Sunita, stunned, nodded his agreement, Buddha helped him to bathe himself and ordained him on the spot. As you can imagine, an uproar ensued. When the local king heard about the incident, he tracked Buddha down to find out what was going on. Had Buddha lost what was left of his mind? But when the king caught a glimpse of Sunita teaching some of the younger monks, he was so moved that he asked for permission to pay Buddha homage instead.

Always on the alert for teaching moments, Buddha used the situation as an introduction to one of his most powerful lessons, the lesson of radiating kindness to all beings: "In the way of liberation there is no caste. To the eyes of the enlightened person all people are equal. Every person's blood is red. Every person's tears are salty. We are all human beings. We must find a way for all people to be able to realize their full dignity and potential." *(Old Path White Clouds)* Everyone is precious. Not most of us. All of us. Everyone—and everything—is sacred.

In another instance, Buddha was visiting a small monastery just outside of the city of Savatthi when he heard a cry of pain coming from one of the huts. Entering it, he found an emaciated monk covered in his own excrement and vomit. The monk had dysentery. When Buddha asked him if anyone was taking care of him, the monk told him that some of the monks had tried to take care of him, but when he realized he was dying he had asked them to just leave him alone to die. Buddha's response was to bathe the monk, change his clothes, and scrub the hut clean. He then boiled some water and sent for some medicine. When the other monks, who had been out on their begging rounds, returned, he talked to them about the courage that is kindness. "If we don't look after each other, who will?" he asked them. It isn't okay to assume that someone else will take care of the problem. If it exists, it is ours. Literally. There is no distance. Any hungry child is our hungry child. A person needing help is us needing help. This is the reality of our lives. To try to hide from suffering is to try to hide from ourselves and our own hearts. When we look away from someone in need, we are breaking our own hearts. And there is more: "Caring for any bhikkhu is the same as caring for the Buddha." *(Old Path White Clouds)* Caring for anyone is caring for the Buddha.

When I first walked through the gates of the Ann Arbor Zen Buddhist Temple, the overwhelming sensation was one of quiet. Only the wind chimes on the front porch offered up any sounds, and theirs were sweet and soft. The people involved in running the temple were open and kind, and there was a bigheartedness about everyone I met. Coming out of the samsaric world at eighty-five miles an hour, I wasn't sure I trusted my own initial reaction. But it kept surrounding me, this impersonal acceptance, even when I was my worst me.

In my first year as a sangha member, I remember rushing in one morning late for a 5 A.M. sitting, disturbing the entire meditation hall with my still slightly drunk, overly boisterous apology. The temple priest, who had left her cushion and walked the length of the hall to open the door for me herself, grinned from ear to ear as she gently steadied me and said, "Oh yes, our mendicant nun is here." She was genuinely pleased to see me, even though my then boyfriend continued to sit in the temple driveway in his massive pick-up truck, positioned so his bright lights could guide my stumbling steps up the temple stairs. The lights were so bright they created a false high noon throughout the building. But there was no judgment, just kindness, that twinkle-in-the-eye kindness that some of us only see in pictures of Santa Claus. It was everywhere.

I asked my daughter, who was six years old at the time, for her reaction to the place. She looked at me, frowning. "You know how most people pretend they're happy?" I nodded. "Over at the temple they really are." And she was right. Over and over I am struck by how real kindness isn't about grandiose actions worthy of prime-time media coverage. It's about small acts that add up: corrections without any judgment; someone noticing that we need help figuring out how to turn on the new digital phone and taking time to show us; someone listening to us without interrupting, appearing beside our car to help carry groceries into the apartment, answering a door promptly, flashing a quick smile.

For several years, whenever I would go to Toronto for a five-day retreat, Samso, the resident priest, would quietly forgo sleep to make sure the rest of us were well fed and cared for. I would see her sneaking around washing towels or dishes when we were all supposed to be resting, or silently making a cup of tea for someone who had found his or her way into the kitchen in the middle of an emotional crisis. Twenty-four hours a day she would radiate this kindness, graciously letting go of opportunity after opportunity for her own quiet contemplation.

And then there is Sunim. In a day-long meeting with seminary students last summer, a woman talked about how she worried so much it got in the way of her practice, which made her worry even more. Upon hearing her words, without skipping a beat, Sunim just looked at her quietly. After several moments, he said, "You can give your worries to me." She nodded. I could see the relief and gratitude as her shoulders relaxed. A few days earlier, he had instructed me to spend twenty-four hours alone in the meditation hall concentrating on "mu" practice. (This is a meditation practice that has become popular recently. Basically, we breathe in deeply and then, while breathing out slowly, we whisper "muuu..." It sounds like wind with an "m" sound regularly interrupting its passage.) I had hit a roadblock in my practice and we both knew it. Project completed, I sat in front of him sobbing from exhaustion and frustration. "I meditated the whole time," I sobbed, trying desperately to understand why the block persisted. "I know," he said, his eyes filled with compassion. He was offering me everything he had, all his wisdom, and his energy. I left the room knowing he would do the same for the next person sitting before him, and the next, and the next.

Radiate kindness. Buddha taught this lesson over and over. Happily, examples surround us. If we look we'll see them and take heart. My friend David Horowitz makes it his personal duty to make sure that none of his single women friends is alone during a holiday, unless it's by choice. Out of the blue he'll take my daughter to dinner or a hockey game, offering her the friendship and mentoring of an unrelated adult as a resource, should she ever need to tap it. He saves her all his *Entertainment Weekly*s and cuts out newspaper articles she might find interesting. I ask Deb Elmore if she knows any electricians who can help a homeless shelter in Detroit, and the next thing I know, she has electricians, plumbers, and carpenters lined up to volunteer their help. And she just happens to have about a room's worth of lighting fixtures she "needs to get rid of."

If Buddha had a best woman friend it was Visakha. She was a feisty and independent-minded lay woman who lived in Savatthi, one of his favorite haunts. Buddha was able to hear things from Visakha that he wasn't willing to hear from his other followers—mostly suggestions for slightly easing the physical difficulties faced by the monks and nuns.

One time when Buddha was about fifty-five years old, he and his monks were invited to dine with Visakha on their arrival at Savatthi for a rainy-season stay. Obtaining permission from Buddha to invite the monks to a meal, Visakha sent her maid into the forest to tell the monks. The first time the maid went into the woods looking for them, all she saw was a bunch of naked men standing in the rain. Figuring they were naked ascetics and not Buddha's followers, she returned to Visakha unaccompanied. Knowing that they were indeed Buddha's followers, Visakha sent the girl back. By this time the rain had stopped and the monks had retired to their huts. Seeing no one, the maid returned home, this time reporting that the forest was empty. Buddha, watching her go back and forth, took pity on her and told the monks to head for Visakha's, where a meal was waiting for all of them.

After Visakha had served food to each of the followers, she sat down next to Buddha and said she had some favors to ask of him. His first reaction? To scold her: "Perfect ones have left favors behind, Visakha." Didn't she know better? Undeterred, the woman kept at him while the rest of the monks looked on, trying not to be stunned by her audacity.

She wanted to give the monks clothes they could wear in the rain. And she wanted to provide food for any monks who visited her on their way through town. Ditto for sick monks and their attendants. She wanted to provide medicine for the monks and keep a constant supply of gruel available. Lastly, she wanted to give the nuns bathing clothes they could wear in the heavy rains so they wouldn't be stuck naked out in public.

Buddha watched her closely while she was asking for the favors. Then he asked her why she wanted to do these things. Emboldened,

Visakha responded: The gruel meant that food would always be available to spiritual seekers. And the sight of all the monks naked in the rain was pretty distracting. As for the visiting monks, her food would give them energy so they could keep up their practice. Without food the sick monks could get sicker, even die. And their attendants, if they were fed by her, would be able to provide better care for them. As for the nuns, they "bathed naked at the same bathing place on the River Aciravati that the harlots used. The harlots made fun of (them), saying, 'Why practice the holy life so young, ladies? Are not sensual desires to be enjoyed? You can live the holy life when you are old. Then you will have the benefit of both.' When the harlots made fun of them thus, the bhikkhunis were put out..." (Bhikkhu Nanamoli, *The Life of the Buddha*, Kandy, Sri Lanka: Buddhist Publication Society, 1992)

The room was silent. Knowing that the monks were closely watching their conversation, Buddha asked the woman what was in it for her. And her answer is our answer, the reason why radiating kindness matters to all of us. "When I remember (a kindness done), I shall be glad. When I am glad, I shall be happy. When my mind is happy, my body will be tranquil. When my body is tranquil, I shall feel pleasure. When I feel pleasure, my mind will become concentrated. That will maintain the spiritual faculties in me and also the spiritual powers and also the enlightenment factors." (*The Life of the Buddha*, p. 155)

Buddha was delighted with her response and promised her that such acts of kindness "lead to heaven, quell sorrow, and bring bliss." He also agreed to let her do as she requested, changing the philosophy of Buddhist practices forever.

Happily, kindness is everywhere. There's a lot more out there than we think. Last weekend, I stopped at a gas station, staring at a red light on my dashboard telling me I needed oil. Instead of just buying some, I walked up to a gorgeous young man filling up his convertible and asked him if he could tell me which motor oil I should buy. I wanted to see if he had any kindness in him. Seeing a scruffy, graying woman about his mother's age, he stopped what he was doing and proceeded to explain the different brands and weights of oil. Then he walked me over to where they were piled and picked the most appropriate one for a 1993 Honda Civic about to face a tough winter. So far, so good.

Then, oil in hand, I walked up to an older gentleman and asked him if he would mind looking over my shoulder while I poured the oil into my car to make certain I did it correctly. He insisted on pouring the oil himself. Finally, on my way out of the gas station, I stopped a young woman with two small children to ask for directions. She drew me a map.

We can rely on each other more than we think. The proof is in our own acts of kindness. One of the initial concerns a surprising number of people have when their spiritual practice really kicks in and they start to downshift their lifestyles is whether their path will lead them straight to an impoverished, homeless life. As a result, I often get asked if I'm afraid of becoming a poor, ancient bag lady. The answer is no. I trust too deeply in all of our hearts, in all of our Buddha natures, and so will you, if you don't already.

Chapter Twelve

❧

Emptying Ourselves of Hatred and Ill Will

"Freed from hatred and ill will"

Tuesday, July 21, 1998

7 A.M.

Journal entry: "Already done: exercise, prostrations, cold shower (ugh), one hour of 'mu' practice. I've decided to live with the birds. When they sleep, I sleep. When they 'mu,' I 'mu.' When they sing, I sing. Seems to be working pretty well. I already have several 'mu' buddies, a couple of flies I've named Harry and Ben and a daddy longlegs by the sink.

"The beauty of this mountaintop is awesome. I am looking out three almost floor-to-ceiling windows at a green field with three huge trees sitting smack in its middle. In the distance, more mountains. Already the weather has changed three times—cloudy, sunny, cloudy. Today in practice I had an insight: that determined effort is only half of our work. We need to let go of our attachments, lighten our obligations, sever the ties that bind. An Asian monk, reacting to Americans meditating, once said that we're like these people sitting in a rowboat who are working incredibly hard. Unfortunately, there is a problem: The rowboat is still tied to the dock.

"I can feel the hanging on. It shows up as flashes of fear or worrying about Jamie and how I struggle with finding the wise way—a place in the middle with her. I still experience flashes of 'I've got to get this right!' The good news is that they are only flashes. Sunim advised me to just meditate and concentrate on 'mu' for these ten days. To just live each twenty-four hours as if it is my whole life. I'm doing that, right now sitting in a cozy old red chair surrounded by posters of Buddhas and Kalu Rinpoche, counting myself as unbelievably lucky."

Determined to cut some ties, I had headed for the woods for ten days to live in a cabin alone with a little food and no visitors. I expected miracles, of course. Maybe the sky would open up and angels might appear—just like the ones on all the Hallmark cards in the holiday season. Instead, I was cursed with thinking, planning, thinking, planning. No room for miracles. When I walked: thinking, planning. When I sat: thinking, planning. After all these years of practice. It was enough to make a grown woman cry. So I did, but even that didn't help. After a couple of days of sheer misery, I remembered that Buddha had just waited out his own fear and despair. I decided to do the same. Hiding my book and my pens, I vowed to just sit.

Day one: whining mind. Poor me. Poor, poor me. This is so stupid. Day two: thinking, less whining. Day three: less thinking, some spaciousness. Day four: spaciousness, some thinking.

Suddenly insights started popping. The first few were hilarious. For a city girl in the woods, the most meaningful one was, "Never blow your nose in an outhouse." Then there was, "Wasps are pretty dumb," followed by the recognition that snakes just want to be forewarned that you are approaching so they can get out of harm's way.

Then I started reseeing past experiences with a new eye, a dharma eye. I began to appreciate lessons people had taught me and I hadn't even known it and that some people walking out of my life was a gift, as was the entrance of others.

I discovered who the real heroes are: us when we are our best selves, and how our best selves are the ones that are openheartedly and fully focused on whatever situation we find ourselves in.

I remembered how, when I first started attending the Zen Buddhist temple's Sunday services, I felt embarrassed all the time. It wasn't that I was sitting incorrectly or snoring when I succumbed to micronaps. It was that the priest, in her dharma talks, was so wide open somehow. She would casually tell stories of her philandering ex-husband who had run off with another woman, or of her struggles with her teenage daughter, or of her frustration with a store clerk who was overcharging her for a drink. She talked about whatever popped up spontaneously. Her talks were always chock full of insights. Sometimes she would have tears in her eyes, sometimes not. And when people attending the service would offer up their understandings of her situations, she was right there with them, nodding as she listened, no space between their words and her heart.

It felt too intimate to me somehow. Almost overwhelming. It was like her arms were wide open to whatever situation she was in—and whatever it brought with it. There was no hatred, no ill will. It was disconcerting. For years I sat there just wishing that she would lecture about the sutras and leave her own life out of it.

Sunim was the same. In every situation he was fully in the eye of its storm without any emotional protections. The rest of us might blink, minds wandering, but not Sunim. He was instantaneously spontaneous in every situation. In one dharma talk he was telling the story of one of his own teachers, a wonderful monk who would occasionally escape the walls of the monastery to visit the local village, and suddenly, in the middle of the dharma talk, Sunim was dancing away, mimicking his teacher's jaunty escape walk.

Later Sunim came to Ann Arbor for a Sunday night on his way to Toronto. We decided to throw an impromptu birthday party for him, not that it was his birthday. The previous exposure Sunim had had of my daughter was when she was about ten years old, small, curly-haired, and shy. Since then, Jamie had morphed into a full-figured swimmer with the broad shoulders of a butterfly stroke fanatic. Quite lovely, she tends to wear her thick black hair in something that looks like a bun, and her face in the evening light becomes Asian. Five years later, as the two of us approached Sunim to greet him, I saw his eyes light on Jamie. "Sumo wrestler!" he exclaimed.

You don't need to be a teenage girl to know that she was hurt. Sunim's reaction to her reaction was immediate. He called at the crack of dawn the next day to tell her that he hadn't meant to hurt her feelings. He explained that this must be a cultural difference between the Midwest and his homeland of Korea. Because he had always been a scrawny little kid growing up, he and the other smaller kids had always been in awe of the bigger, stronger kids. He hoped she understood that his reaction was a compliment in his world.

Sunim had a temple full of other priorities to attend to but it didn't matter. Jamie was what was right in front of him. I was struck by Sunim's complete immersion in the situation. There wasn't anything else in his life except the interaction with Jamie. We all need to get there, to that no-thinking mind.

On some days, the woods where I was staying felt like a petting zoo. There were deer, snakes, rabbits galore, a red fox, a couple of dogs, pheasants, and rumors of a black bear. By day five they were mostly used to me and I was mostly used to them. Then one morning, I was walking along a footpath, the woods to my left and a field to my right. Suddenly the air was filled with cries that sounded like ducks in trouble. Out of nowhere popped up adorable and furry baby somethings. A dozen or so were scurrying away from me, half on either side of the path.

In the same instant there was a bloodcurdling screech right behind me. I turned around. About ten feet away was a wild turkey headed straight at me. Let me tell you that those suckers are big, and with its wings spread out it looked huge and mad.

Without thinking I spun on my heels, faced it square on and shouted, "Back off! This isn't just your path!" We were both stunned. The turkey slammed on its brakes and stared at me for a couple of seconds. I stared back. Then it walked over to the field and nudged its babies toward a safer, more secluded spot. I continued on my way, thinking, "Wow, this stuff really works." Five days earlier I would have run to my car, jumped in, and driven back to the city where it's safe. Instead, in the middle of deep practice, a thought-less response surfaced in a way that protected us both.

After those days of concentrated practice, I realized with a jolt that all of my fears were gone, maybe for the first time in my whole life. There was literally no fear—not of poverty, not of pain, not of aging. No fear of being alone. Or with people. No fear of death. And with the fear went all of my anger and ill will. Gone. All of it. I realized that old Morrie, in *Tuesdays with Morrie,* was right. That a meaningful life is about loving other people and devoting myself to this crazy world that is home. And I had to grin, thinking about his words to his student, Mitch Albom, which Mitch muses on here:

> Remember what I said about finding a meaningful life? I wrote it down, but now I can recite it: Devote yourself to loving others, devote yourself to your community around you, and devote yourself to creating something that gives you purpose and meaning. ...There's nothing in there about a salary. I jotted some of the things Morrie was saying on a yellow pad. I did this mostly because I didn't want him to see my eyes, to know what I was thinking, that I had been, for much of my life since graduation, pursuing these very things he had been railing against— bigger toys, nicer house. Because I worked among rich and famous athletes, I convinced myself that my needs were realistic, my greed inconsequential compared to theirs.
>
> (Mitch Albom, *Tuesday with Morrie: An Old Man, a Young Man, and the Last Great Lesson,* New York: Doubleday, 1997)

What a teacher Mitch Albom had in Morrie:

> He paused, then looked at me. "I'm dying, right?"
>
> "Yes."
>
> "Why do you think it's so important for me to hear other people's problems? Don't I have enough pain and suffering on my own?
>
> "Of course I do. But giving to other people is what makes me feel alive. Not my car or my house. Not what I look like in the mirror. When I give my time, when I can make someone smile after they were feeling sad, it's as close to healthy as I ever feel.
>
> "Do the kinds of things that come from the heart. When you do you won't be dissatisfied, you won't be envious, you won't be longing for somebody else's things. On the contrary, you'll be overwhelmed by what comes back."

(Tuesdays with Morrie)

On that path with that turkey, swimming in spaciousness, the pieces of the puzzle fell into place. I realized that nothing was missing in my life. Nothing.

It took a while to notice I was dancing all the way down that mountain and then all the way back. Down again. Up again. Again and again.

꙰

Chapter Thirteen

Why Vows Matter

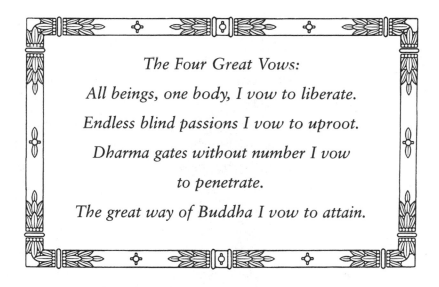

The Four Great Vows:

All beings, one body, I vow to liberate.

Endless blind passions I vow to uproot.

Dharma gates without number I vow

to penetrate.

The great way of Buddha I vow to attain.

It's not that I consciously sit next to couples in coffee shops who are casually breaking up eight-year relationships, but it keeps happening. Five times in four months, actually. I started counting after the second couple. Each time I am stunned at how easily the two people are willing to let go. These are multiyear relationships. For some of that time they must have been deeply meaningful or they wouldn't have lasted. Yet I hear years of life passages erased with quips and jokes and "Well, we tried." One woman said to her partner, "I'm so happy that we've both grown up. Now maybe we can find real relationships." Hmmm.

Just as I started obsessing about the scary state of relationships, I began to notice another recent behavioral pattern—people reneging on promises as if they had never really mattered. I'm seeing this more and more often in the business world. Colleagues not calling when they said they would. No explanations later. Scheduled meetings with RSVPs where people didn't bother to show up. In one instance, four consultants had flown to Michigan from the East Coast to meet a CEO who hadn't bothered to come into the office that day, let alone show up for his own session.

Last September I was flying home to Detroit from New Jersey, and two men sitting right behind me spent the entire flight plotting how they could get out of doing something they had promised for a client. At the end of the trip one of them said, "I don't think we need to worry about it...he's probably forgotten anyway. Let's just see if he says anything." A week later, on my way back to New Jersey on a 7 A.M. flight crammed full of sleep-deprived and caffeine-withdrawn passengers, a young woman actually picked up the phone embedded in the seat ahead of her and proceeded to call her sister to tell her she had to move out that night, "because it just isn't working...no big reason...it just isn't," while the rest of us listened and some of us cringed.

So here's the question: When did we become these shrugging "whatever" machines? When did we decide that halfhearted efforts were enough, that promises were words of intention, not commitment? Was it the year we thought about trying a diet, instead of actually shifting our eating habits until we shed some weight? Did it start in the 1960s, when a whole generation of us decided it was okay to try out living with someone instead of making a long-term commitment which included sticking out the tough times that invariably occur? Did technology teach us simply to log off when life skews off-center the same way we log off when something unpleasant appears on our computer screens?

Something has been lost. I think of my grandparents. My grandfather was this huge (to a small child, anyway) German baker from Bavaria who was stern and quiet and efficient. I don't remember him singing, or playing, even. He was just there. I don't remember him hugging us or kissing us. Instead, he would take us for walks in Boston every time we visited. Long walks to gardens, to ponds, to baseball games, to the ice cream store. It was his passion, this walking. Every day he would walk for miles and miles when he was finished baking through the night. And take us all along, if we were visiting. It gave him pleasure, he said. And it was true.

My grandmother, his wife, was a teeny, spunky Irish woman. She would do anything for her family, including giving each of her grandchildren an entire pie to eat on our own terms whenever we visited the bakery she owned with my grandfather. She worked, she smiled, she worked, she smiled, she worked. Theirs was a mismatch that even I could see. And yet they took their marriage vows seriously. When my grandmother got sick, my grandfather nursed her, and when her nephews got drunk, really drunk, he bailed them out of trouble. When he got diabetes, she nursed him, and when they cut off his legs to save his life, she would take walks for him, telling him the news of the day—which ducks had babies, the kind of ice cream they were selling at the park. Until he died. Because she had promised that only death would part them.

Vows. I bought my first car when I was thirty. I had managed, until then, to live in cities such as New York, where public transportation made car ownership unnecessary, for students anyway. Then I moved to Oregon and needed a car, so I bought one from a fellow graduate student—a little Volvo. I realized, after he dropped it off, that I had no idea how to shift gears. To teach myself, I drove all over the place, grinding gears, stalling, and making many of Portland's drivers wish (sometimes openly) that I would move back to wherever I had come from. After a couple of weeks I decided to polish my skills by driving to California, to Disneyland. I had never been there and it promised to be a beautiful drive. Although I spent several hundred miles in first gear trying to perfect my shifting technique, the trip to Disneyland was uneventful. On the way back, however, the car died in the middle of a desert with nobody and nothing in sight—only desert.

With miles of nothing behind me and no idea how far away the nearest gas station was ahead of me, I sat in the car crying because that's what

I do. And while the fatalistic part of me decided to review my life just in case it was my last day on earth, the more alert part of me watched an enormous fancy Buick pull up behind the Volvo. The driver got out and asked if he could help.

I told him my car had died. He nodded and proceeded to look at all the car sections that people who know something about cars look at. Then he came to my window and said, "Could be." Told me to put the car in neutral and he would push me to the nearest gas station.

It was forty-two miles away. When we got there, it turned out that there was hope for the car, after all. Miracle of miracles, there was a motel next door where I could spend the night while the mechanics brought the car back to life. As my savior, who never told me his name, turned to leave the gas station, confident that I was okay, I asked him why he had stopped. He told me that he had made a vow never to drive past a person on the highway who was in trouble. Maybe he saved my life.

Vows. Buddhism is a world of vows. When Buddha gave up his princely life at twenty-nine to become an ascetic in search of the answer to all of our suffering, he made a lot of people unhappy. His wife was left to raise a child on her own. His father, who had purposefully groomed Buddha to take over the management of his property, was devastated. His stepbrother missed him deeply, as did his stepmother, who had raised him from the time he was born. As you can imagine, it took Buddha some years, after his enlightenment, to return to his family for a visit.

When he did, his family, who had been following his progress, was thrilled to see him, and any anger they had harbored fell away as they realized the truth of his wisdom. Even his son Rahula, who was an adolescent, wanted to join him as a monk. Buddha turned him down, instead offering specific guidelines for how to grow into manhood. Years later, Rahula was finally ready to become a monk.

And Buddha's advice hardened in those years. Where he had been advising the young Rahula to try to be like the earth, accepting all things without judgment, or to try to be like water, or wind, he told the adult

Rahula to make vows he would keep, no matter what. Like Yoda, he told Rahula that there is no *try*, there is only *do*. Here are his words to his son: "Practice loving-kindness to get rid of ill will. Practice compassion to get rid of cruelty. Practice sympathy to get rid of apathy. Practice equanimity to get rid of resentment....Practice contemplation of impermanence to get rid of the conceit 'I am.' Practice mindfulness of breathing; for when that is maintained in being and well developed, it brings great fruit and many blessings." (Bhikkhu Nanamoli, *The Life of the Buddha,* Kandy, Sri Lanka: Buddhist Publication Society, 1992)

Buddha's instructions were not "consider these things," they were "do these things." To vow it. When we perform the four great vows at the temple, we don't say, "All beings, one body, I will try to liberate," or "I will think about trying to liberate." We say, "All beings, one body, I vow to liberate." We vow to uproot our endless blind passions. We vow to attain the great way of Buddha. We are promising to give our spiritual work everything we've got, and then some. Because that is what it takes and because we can. There's something about someone making a vow that makes us sit up straight and listen. Our respect blossoms. Recently I was with a friend in another temple. One night he went out for dinner and drinks, coming back late. The next day he was pretty fuzzy. At a temple meeting he was asked why he drank. His response was simple. To vow to stop drinking. It was a problem for him, he knew it was a problem, and he was ready to stop. We witnessed his promise, and I secretly pledged to do everything I could to help him keep his vow. Because it mattered.

Shortly thereafter, I was lucky enough to witness a second set of vows. One of my dharma brothers, Paramita, and his family were on a whirlwind visit from Japan to friends and family in the United States. Paramita had rewritten the four great vows as vows of self-acceptance and asked that Sukha, the temple priest, and I witness his recitation of them in the meditation hall. I was moved beyond words that he had thought about the four great vows so deeply and had taken the time to translate them into guidelines aimed at reaching the core of his own experience and spirituality. I was moved that he was willing to share his wisdom with us and openly promise everything to the accomplishment of the four vows.

I'll tell you a secret. Without making and keeping a vow to keep up your spiritual practice, you're a goner. Sloth will move in faster than you can ask, "What's on TV tonight?" It is too easy to slide. The distractions are too powerful. Without a vow to keep up your practice, how will you get up on a cold morning to do prostrations or meditate? Even knowing the value of both, they wither and die without a commitment. Without a vow, how do any of us actually start living our practice every moment, all the time instead of some of the time, instead of when we feel like it?

Without a vow to keep our hearts sincere and our compassion strong, we can be subtly overwhelmed with our own anger, greed, and delusion. It can happen so quickly, we may not even notice until we have hurt someone else or slipped into the land of "whatever." Without vows, how can we stay true to our friends, our family, all beings? The truth is, we can't. We need that man to stop on the highway. And he needs us. And we need to be there for our partner who has suffered greatly. And he needs to be there for us. And I haven't even started on our relationships with animals, nature, and the rest of the universe.

Here's another secret. When we make a vow and stick to it, we accept ourselves. We start to understand the peace that comes with living a life of integrity, where we don't have to worry about what we might have done by breaking a commitment. **We trust other people more, because if we can keep a vow, they can too.**

So make some vows. Start with one. And start small. The momentum will carry itself.

Here are a few to choose from, if you don't have your own ideas:

I vow to pick up three pieces of litter each day.

I vow to be home for dinner each night by 6:30 P.M.

I vow to tell my son I love him every day.

I vow to call my mother once a week.

I vow to put healthier foods in my mouth.

I vow to be true to my mate.

I vow to experience the divine.

I vow to laugh at least once a day.

Start. Your life could be over tomorrow. Do you really want to waste another minute? In the Jewish mystical tradition I am told there is a belief that any time a good deed is done, an angel is born. Just imagine what we can do with vows. We'll need another planet, we'll be so crowded.

Whether standing or walking, seated or lying down
Free from drowsiness,
One should sustain this recollection.

May all beings be happy.